FOURTH EDITION

The First Year: Making the Most of College

GLENDA A. BELOTE
LARRY W. LUNSFOR
Florida International Univ

D1379036

KENDALL/HUNT PUBLISHING COMPANY
4050 Westmark Drive Dubuque, Iowa 52002

Copyright © 1996, 1998, 2001, 2003 by Kendall/Hunt Publishing Company

ISBN 0-7575-0226-1

Printed in the United States of America

10 9 8 7 6 5 4 3

CONTENTS

ACKNOWLEDGMENTS

This is the fourth edition of *The First Year: Making the Most of College.* There are a number of additions and changes that reflect both changing information and feedback from students, instructors, and colleagues. As always, we appreciate the time others have taken to provide us with their thoughts and observations on the first-year experience course and this text.

Chapter five, on information literacy, originally prepared by Patricia Iannuzzi, has been substantially rewritten by Dr. Elizabeth J. McNeer with an emphasis on the use of computers in academic research and the classroom. Dr. Robert Dollinger, Executive Director of University Health Services, has revised Chapter 8, "Maintaining a Healthy Lifestyle," and Dr. Beverly Dalrymple, Director of the Center for Leadership and Civic Responsibility, has made additions and changes to Chapter 9, "Planning for a Career." All are strong advocates for the course and generous contributors to this edition of the text.

A number of colleagues have offered materials, ideas, insights, and suggestions over the years. Included are Janie Valdes, Kathy Trionfo, Dr. William Keppler, and Dr. John Bonanno. Many of these colleagues continue to regularly teach the first-year experience course and remain actively involved in the academic and personal development of students.

The Publications Office at Florida International University under the direction of Bill Stahl provided the photographs for this and previous editions. We are particularly grateful to Allison Einhorn-Perez for her assistance in locating within their extensive files the types of student and faculty images we wanted to represent in this revision.

To all who have contributed both formally and informally, we appreciate your insights and expertise, your acceptance, always with good grace, of our editorial comments and decisions, and your willingness to almost always meet the deadlines we established so arbitrarily! We continue to value you as friends and colleagues.

Larry W. Lunsford
Assistant Vice President, Student
Affairs, and University Ombudsman

Glenda A. Belote
Associate Dean, Undergraduate Studies

Introduction

When Robert Louis Stevenson was a boy, he sat by the window at dusk one evening quietly watching the lamplighter as he walked by his house touching the gas wick to the gaslights on his street. His mother, concerned over the long period of silence, asked young Robert what he was doing. He replied, "I am watching the man punch holes in the darkness."

Welcome to the University • • • • • •

Do you remember when you were younger how often you were asked, "What do you want to be when you grow up?" Now, with your enrollment in the university, you will finally begin the process of answering that question as you select your major and define a career path for yourself.

To assist you with your adjustment to the university environment, this course and textbook are considered important starting points. Many students find the transition from high school to college is easy; for others, however, the first year of college is a stressful and sometimes frustrating experience. **Your** experience in college will be exactly what **you** want it to be. If you start college with a negative attitude or don't really want to be here, then you most likely will not achieve academic success. If you begin this year with enthusiasm and an openness to new learning, both inside the classroom and through the variety of new experiences available to you on campus, then college may be the best time of your life!

This course is designed to help prepare you to meet the challenges you will face in this academic environment. The objectives of the course are to assist students in: developing skills which will support academic achievement; developing an understanding of complex choices and issues confronting a college student; managing the university environment in ways that will encourage completion of a degree; understanding resources and services available on campus; and, understanding basic academic requirements, policies, and procedures.

We hope the course will also assist you in making the many adjustments necessary to succeed in college: note taking skills, test taking skills, information literacy skills, meeting and working with professors and other students, time management, balancing responsibilities and multiple roles, and developing an appreciation for differences. You will find the course requires participation by you as you explore the issues and topics presented.

The text is designed to be user-friendly! Write in it! Underline or highlight important information! Tear out pages and make copies of useful forms! The more you use this text, the more you will gain from it. The exercises will provide you with both a better understanding of the ideas presented and an opportunity for you to assess who you are and where you are headed. Self-awareness is an important database upon which to build your college experiences.

The instructor for this course knows the university and its policies and procedures. Your instructor also teaches this course because he or she has an interest in seeing you succeed in college. Get to know your instructor; visit in her office. Ask him questions when you are not sure what to do or where to go. For many students, their instructor becomes a resource beyond this class and this term.

Remember, college is what **YOU** make of it. Decisions you make now will influence the direction of your life in the future; friends you make now will, in many cases, become friends for life. Things will not always be easy and you shouldn't want it that way. When you work hard and earn your way, you will place greater value on your education. Work toward academic success, but also remember to take time to enjoy what college life has to offer outside of the classroom.

First Year Experience SLS 1501 Common Syllabus • • • • • •

Purpose: The purpose of this course is to introduce students to the university and provide information that will promote and support academic success. The course includes a review of basic skills and competencies necessary to college success, including, but not limited to, time management, study skills, and an orientation to university policies and procedures. In addition, important topics such as alcohol and drugs, AIDS, and acquaintance rape are also included.

Objectives: Objectives of the course are to assist students in:

1. developing skills which will support academic achievement,
2. developing an understanding of the complex issues and choices confronting a college student,
3. managing the university environment in ways that support completion of an academic degree,
4. understanding the resources and services available on campus, and
5. understanding basic academic requirements, policies and procedures.

Text: **The First Year: Making the Most of College,** by Glenda A. Belote and Larry W. Lunsford.

The text is both a workbook and a compilation of useful readings. It is required that each student purchase a personal copy. Used texts are not available because of the workbook format.

Campus Involvement: Involvement in the campus community is an important part of campus life. All students must select and participate in three events, programs, or activities outside the classroom. Selected experiences may not be a part of requirements for another course. A list of possible activities will be provided.

Examinations: There will be a final examination, semester project, or portfolio required. Each instructor will announce which option will be used in his/her section. In addition, each instructor will give quizzes or a mid-term examination. Each instructor will announce his/her quiz policy including the number of quizzes, grading, and make-up opportunities, if any. **Requirements may vary from section to section.**

Office Interviews: Contact with instructors outside the classroom is important in college. Students are encouraged to meet with the course instructor at least once to review academic progress, discuss questions of concern to the student, or talk about any topics of interest to the student. **Some instructors may require an individual interview with some or all students in the class.**

Written Work: Each instructor will define expectations for written assignments, including workbook exercises, journals, and papers. **Assignments may vary from section to section.**

Grading: Each instructor will describe his/her grading policies and system. A final examination, project or portfolio, quizzes, and campus involvement are required for all students. Other assignments may vary from section to section.

Course Topics: Instructors will select assignments from among the topics listed below. Assigned readings and written work may vary from section to section because instructors emphasize different materials from the text.

At the first class session, all instructors will go over the following information: syllabus, attendance policy, text, general expectations, getting acquainted.

Because of time constraints, not all listed topics can be covered. Possible topics for the term include:

1. The campus environment and resources
2. Time management
3. Note taking
4. Faculty teaching styles
5. Diversity and appreciation for differences
6. Core curriculum and advising
7. Test-taking strategies
8. Developing relationships
9. Campus policies and procedures
10. Listening and memory skills
11. Managing financial resources
12. Health/wellness
13. Critical thinking
14. Choosing a major
15. Preparing for finals
16. Reading and analyzing
17. Cults

CHAPTER 1

Getting to Know the Campus

*"Be the change you want to
see in the world."*
—Gandhi

Starting the Year Right • • • • • • • • •

Starting the year right as a first year student often determines how well your first semester, and perhaps your first year, will go for you. For example, if you don't purchase the books for your classes until several weeks into the semester, you may find that one or more of the books you need are no longer available. You may also learn that you are already too far behind to catch up.

The following recommendations are a useful guide in "Starting the Year Right" and remaining on the right track during your first semester at FIU. Review this checklist periodically to ensure that you are staying current with the recommendations.

Before Classes Begin . . .

- Get to know the campus and where things are.
- Look over the **Undergraduate Catalog** and **Student Handbook.**
- Read a copy of **The Beacon** (the student newspaper).
- Review your class schedule.

During the First Week of Classes . . .

- Buy your textbooks.
- Set up a notebook for classes.
- Get an appointment book and use it.
- Attend all of your classes.
- Meet at least one new person.

During the First Month of the Year . . .

- Attend all your classes.
- Get to classes on time.
- Make sure you know how to use the library.
- Post all of your assignment deadlines in your calendar.
- Participate in class.

By the End of the Term . . .

- Have all your assignments completed and turned in.
- Have a study schedule set for final exams.
- Have your registration completed for the next term.
- Start planning your next term's commitments (work, etc.).
- Evaluate what changes you need to make for next term.

Getting Involved • • • • • • • • • • • • • • •

Why should you get involved on campus? You're carrying a heavy class load, working part-time, and commuting from home. Where are you supposed to find extra time to join a club or organization and stay late for meetings on campus? What good does co-curricular involvement do anyway? After all, aren't you here just to study, get good grades, graduate, and get a nice job?

At some point in their academic career, all students (particularly freshmen) probably ask themselves these questions. It is wise that you ask the questions so that you understand why some co-curricular involvement can be as important to your academic success as what you learn in the classroom.

In this chapter, you'll learn more about why it is important to get involved on campus and how this involvement can make you a better student as well as enhance your future employment or graduate and professional school opportunities.

To reinforce the importance of campus and community involvement, during this course you will be required to select three campus involvement activities as part of the requirements. You may want to select an activity in which you already have an interest, but you might also consider an activity which is new and will help broaden your education. Your instructor will discuss possible activities in greater detail.

You might also consider getting involved in the community. The Volunteer Action Center (VAC) coordinates student volunteer activities on campus. The VAC has two central focuses. First, they coordinate and direct service-learning activities on campus. Second, they act as a clearinghouse and resource center for volunteer opportunities and advocacy in the community.

Textbooks • • • • • • • • • • • • • • • • • • •

Would you ever jump off a high diving board into a swimming pool if you couldn't swim? Not likely. If you wouldn't do that, then why would you attend university classes without buying the required textbooks?

Classroom learning involves many dimensions, including lectures by instructors, active participation by students, and reading assigned material in the textbook. The textbook reinforces what is taught in class. In fact, some professors base their lectures strictly on material from the text.

At the beginning of this chapter, one of the top recommendations for things to do during the first week of school is to buy your textbooks. This is important because most of your classes will have textbook assignments given during the first class meeting. The longer you wait to buy your books, the further behind you will fall in assigned readings. Don't start the year by getting behind! You may find it difficult, and perhaps impossible, to catch up as each new assignment is added.

Another result of not buying your books early is that the campus bookstore may not have enough texts in stock to meet demand. This means you will have to share a textbook with a willing classmate to keep up with assignments, if you wait until more books are ordered, you may be weeks behind in your reading.

A fair warning: textbooks are not cheap! Depending on the course, size of the book, and whether or not it is a paperback or hardback, texts can cost from a few dollars to over $100. Both new and used texts are available in the bookstore. You might find students or other sources selling used books cheaper than the campus bookstore. However, make sure that if you purchase a book from anyone other than the bookstore that you are buying the correct edition that will be used in the class. Books may appear to be the same, but newer editions contain information not included in older editions.

At the end of the semester, you may choose to sell your books back to the bookstore, or you may decide to keep certain books to start or add to your personal library. Please note that the campus bookstore buys back your books for much less than you paid for them, and the store does not buy back all books. Some texts are discontinued, while others may be in poor condition and cannot be resold.

The Syllabus • • • • • • • • • • • • • • • • • •

It is expected that most, if not all, of your instructors will provide you with a copy of the syllabus for the class the first day or week of classes. A syllabus is a synopsis of information you need to know about the class. It is the professor's written description of the class and may include course expectations, the attendance policy, the grading policy, reading assignments, test and quiz dates, the professor's name, office location, and phone number, and a session-by-session listing of assignments. The common syllabus for this course was included in the introductory section. Your instructor will add his own syllabus addendum with more information specific to his expectations.

It is important that you review the syllabus prior to each class session so that you know the assignment, what topics will be discussed, and whether or not homework is due. Most importantly, the syllabus informs you well in advance of important dates when tests will be given or papers will be due so that you can adequately study, conduct research, or prepare for exams. The syllabus may also list holidays and other days when class will not meet so that you won't show up and be the only one there!

If you have a class in which a syllabus is not provided, be sure to ask the instructor for all of the information normally included in the syllabus. You may need to do this at each class meeting so that you know reading assignments, homework, and test dates.

Campus Resources • • • • • • • • • • • • •

Your classmates will become one of the more valuable resources you will have in college. It is important that you get to know one or more people in every class. Be sure to get their names and phone numbers should you ever need to contact them.

There are several reasons why you may need to contact a classmate. Should you miss a class, you can call a classmate to learn what you missed, and what assignments were given, and possibly to borrow their class notes. It is advisable to call your instructor, too, when you know you are going to miss a class.

Getting to know your classmates is also a good way of making new friends. College is an exciting time, and it is nice to share the excitement with others who are experiencing the same feelings as you. In an emergency situation, you will find it valuable to be able to contact someone in each of your classes, particularly if you have difficulty reaching an instructor.

Another valuable aspect of meeting your classmates is to form a study group that can assist each member of the group, particularly in your harder classes. Study groups are discussed further in the next chapter.

Exercise 1.1 will assist you in starting to know some of the students in your First Year Experience class. Try to meet as many new people as possible in completing the exercise.

While classmates can be useful in various ways, be cautious when asking opinions about what courses or instructors to take. Everyone learns differently and because one of your friends did not like a course or a particular instructor does not mean that you will share the same opinion. Ask several students for their opinions and recommendations about instructors and courses or read the evaluations of instructors that are on file in the university library so that you will be well informed before making your decisions.

One of the best aspects of attending college is gaining and developing independence in decision making. Be sure to take this opportunity to create your own opinions through careful analysis of problems you face and decisions you make. Another point to consider: you also assume **responsibility** for the choices you make, both good and bad!

Your Professors • • • • • • • • • • • • • • • • • •

It always amazes us how many students don't know the names of their professors, even at the end of the semester. Further, it is likely that these same students have never conversed with a professor outside of class.

Not only is it important that you get to know your classmates, but you need to meet your professors. Don't wait until you are having difficulty with the class or run into a problem to make contact. If your professor already knows you **before** you approach her with a problem, she may be more sympathetic to your situation.

Professors can be your most valuable resource on campus, so use them wisely. Ask questions and participate regularly during class. Students are often afraid to ask questions because they believe that they are the only ones in the class who don't know the answers.

Remember, there are no ridiculous questions! You are in college to gain knowledge, and asking questions is one key ingredient to learning.

You should also visit your professors during their office hours to obtain additional assistance. You need to investigate all possible means of enhancing your academic potential. Tapping this faculty resource is a sure way of getting ahead.

You will learn early in your college transition that college professors are different than your high school teachers. Although there are exceptions, you may find that some college professors seem less personable than your high school teachers; you see them much less during each week and there isn't the same opportunity to get to know each other as well. College classes are often much larger than in high school. In order to get to know your professors better, ask questions and participate in class, and visit them during office hours. Your extra effort could be rewarded once your professors compute grades at semester's end.

Fill in the information in Exercise 1.2 so you have a handy reference of the names, phone numbers, and office locations of your current professors. Complete this form before the end of the first week of the semester.

Other Important People • • • • • • • •

There are many other individuals who will become valuable resources for you. As you have done with your classmates and faculty, get to know as many other people on campus as you can. You will be surprised how helpful these "contacts" are when you run into a problem.

Your contacts could include someone in the Financial Aid Office, Registrar's Office, Student Government Association, Academic Advising Center, Public Safety, Athletics, or a secretary or receptionist in an academic department or other university office. "Networking" is something you'll often do after graduation, so be sure to get in a little practice while you're an undergraduate.

Last, but not least, get to know the campus student leaders. Meet your elected college representative to the Student Government Council or the students who serve as club officers. These individuals and other student leaders are responsible for representing the interests of their peers to the administration, and they, too, can be valuable resources in your quest for academic success.

How Do I Approach a Professor? • • •

People who teach the classes you take vary widely. Some are full professors; others may be graduate students. Although there is no official protocol in approaching your professors, it is common courtesy to follow certain procedures regardless of who teaches the class.

Your instructors have various titles. It is helpful to know whether or not your instructor has completed a doctorate. If so, you should address him or her as "Dr." Otherwise, you may call the individual Mr., Mrs., or Ms., depending on the person's preference. Some professors will tell you how they prefer to be addressed; others will not. It is best to err on the formal side in the absence of any information.

Individuals who teach classes have an academic rank. They may be professors, assistant professors, associate professors, or instructors. "Adjunct" or part-time instructors are individuals who are not full-time members of an academic department but are hired to teach on a temporary basis, usually by the semester. Adjunct professors are fully qualified to teach in the university even though their appointments are temporary.

Most of your professors have regular office hours and will give you their office location and phone number. Sometimes you can just drop by their office, but it is best to make an appointment in advance or call first to see if the individual is available. You may also ask a professor after class if you can speak with him then, or make an appointment. Some professors may give you their home phone number to call if you have an emergency. Make sure you call a professor at home only if it is absolutely necessary!

Try not to be intimidated about asking for help. All professors ultimately want to help students understand the material. It is to your benefit to get to know your professors, especially in your large classes, in order to convey your desire to learn and keep up your grades.

Do not wait until the week before midterms or final examinations to approach a professor about difficulties you are having in class. Get to know your instructors from the beginning so that it doesn't seem like you are approaching them only because you have a problem. Demonstrating an interest throughout the semester may prove to be beneficial for you at the end of the semester when your professors calculate grades.

If you use a cell phone or beeper, turn it off before class. Beepers and cell phones are disruptive in the classroom and suggest you are not a serious student.

Some professors will make you leave the classroom if your beeper beeps or phone rings. We know one professor who will not let a student return to class unless she or he meets privately with the professor and has a good reason for disrupting the lecture and other students.

The Line of Authority • • • • • • • • •

At some point in your college career, you may believe you were treated badly by a professor or that you received an unfair grade. It is important for you to first address the problem with the professor. Rarely will a professor's supervisor meet with a student regarding a complaint unless the student has first met with the professor.

If you meet with a professor and still believe that the problem was not addressed to your satisfaction, you may make an appointment to see the professor's supervisor. The person you see next will probably be a department chairperson. The normal chain of command is as follows: faculty—department chair—dean of the college—provost—president of the university.

Some departments may have a formal method for filing complaints, so check with the department's secretary to determine the procedure to follow. Also note that each of the individuals in the chain of command may have an assistant or associate to whom you may be referred. This may seem like a lot of red tape, but don't let it discourage you! You have the right to be heard, and you have the right to appeal to a higher authority when you believe you have been treated unjustly.

In situations involving academic appeals or alleged academic misconduct, there are specific procedures outlined in the **Student Handbook**. Review these policies and procedures if you have a complaint or are accused of academic misconduct.

The Student Handbook and Undergraduate Catalog • • • • • • • • •

The **Student Handbook** and **Undergraduate Catalog** are two of the most important books you'll get—and you don't even have to pay for them! The **Undergraduate Catalog** is published every year and is available in the Admissions Office. Freshman and transfer students are given both the **Undergraduate Catalog** and **Student Handbook** at Orientation. If you don't have a copy of the **Student Handbook**, you can get one in the Campus Life office.

The **Student Handbook** is a handy reference book containing information about many aspects of the university. The table of contents lists what the handbook contains and on what page you can find that information. It also contains a calendar which you can use to note appointments and other information. The calendar lists important information for you to know, such as registration dates, drop and add deadlines, and other relevant academic dates.

You will find information about most offices and departments in this handbook as well as the location and phone number for the office or department.

The **Student Handbook** also contains the university's Student Conduct Codes and Academic Policies. A word to the wise: become familiar with these sections so that you know a little about the policies before you are faced with a potential problem. Information on academic dishonesty is also found in the **Student Handbook**. Read through the **Student Handbook** and keep it readily available at any time you need to look up various information.

The **Undergraduate Catalog** lists the academic calendar, programs, policies, requirements, and regulations of the university. Descriptions of all courses, departments, faculty, and degree requirements are also found in this book.

Basic information on such areas as admissions, registration, academic regulations, and financial aid is included. The course descriptions can be used to assist students in selecting classes as well as learning prerequisites and choosing potential majors.

Obstacles •

As you journey through your first year of college, you will encounter occasional obstacles along the way. You are not alone! Every new student encounters some problems in mastering the academic routine: college may be harder than you expected; you'll have trouble making new friends; you may feel homesickness or have difficulty getting along with a roommate; personal or family problems may occur; there may be financial difficulty or work conflicts; you may experience test anxiety or bad grades; or, perhaps you might find that college is not sufficiently challenging. Remember, no problem exists that some student hasn't previously faced. It's how you address the problem and come through it that is important. Don't give up and quit! Meet the challenge and tell yourself that you can do it. Solving problems and getting past obstacles are also part of the learning process and will assist you later in your professional life. Did you not have problems in high school? You made it through them, and you will successfully address any obstacles you face in college as well.

Traps for Unsuspecting Students • • •

In the coming weeks and months, some campus organizations may invite you to join them. The majority of these groups are well-meaning and constructive, whether they are religious, self-improvement, volunteer service, cultural, or social in nature.

There are also individuals and groups on campus who would like to share more of their "ideas" with you. Members of these groups may approach you after class, in the residence hall, in the University Center, in the library, or elsewhere on campus, particularly if you are sitting by yourself. In addition to sharing with you the answers they have found to life's questions, they may seek to enlist your time, energy, and resources in endeavors they believe to be worthwhile. They may invite you to a weekend retreat or meeting. In short, they may ask you to join their group and, in the process, make substantial contributions of your time and money to their organization.

Although it is healthy for groups to further their causes and increase membership, some use recruiting tactics that are deceitful, manipulative, harassing, or coercive. Legitimate groups, including religious groups, will tell you a lot about themselves right in the beginning—who they are, what they stand for, and what they expect from you. An open and responsible group will offer an easy entrance to, and, more importantly, an easy exit from the group. Within legitimate groups, one finds an appreciation of diversity, individualism, and openness to criticism and doubt, and an affirmation of differing views and traditions.

Unfortunately there are several groups on campus, both formal and informal, that use high-pressure recruiting practices. Some of these groups may actually be cults or cult-like in their activities. Students are specific targets for their "sales pitch".

Don't be fooled by:

- Instant and intense friendship from a stranger.
- High pressure tactics to get involved immediately.
- An unusual personal interest in you.

Don't:

- Give out your name, address, or phone number to strangers.
- Give personal information about you or your family.
- Leave campus alone with anyone or any group you don't know.
- Contribute money to any group without knowing a lot about them.

Do:

- Ask for the person's name.
- Ask about the organization's goals and purposes.
- Ask questions about what the group does.
- Report any contacts which make you uncomfortable.
- Say no! You are under no obligation to become involved.

High-pressure groups are harmful because they:

- Try to isolate you from your family, friends, and other groups.
- Ask and expect you to give up control of your life, thoughts, and decisions.
- Purposely promote crises with school, career, or your "love life."
- Use mind control or brainwashing techniques in indoctrinating new members.

Could this happen to you? It has happened to other students. However, it is less likely to occur if you are aware and take the time to ask questions and evaluate groups carefully. Legitimate campus and student groups are usually registered on campus and are known to staff in the Campus Life office or student organizations office. Check out groups that interest you if you have any questions or concerns.

Figure 1.1 Definition of Terms

Here are some definitions of commonly used terms, policies, or procedures you may hear about or need to refer to in the coming weeks and months.

Advanced Placement (AP) Credits: Credits earned by taking a national examination in a particular subject area while in high school.

Catalog: Book published by the university which contains important information regarding majors, academic policies, and various services on campus. Students are given a catalog at the Orientation program or may pick up a copy from the Admissions Office or the Registrar's Office.

CLAST (College Level Academic Skills Test): A state-wide achievement test which measures selected communication and computational skills in four sub-tests: essay, English language skills, reading, and mathematics. All students must pass the CLAST or qualify for exemption by meeting one of the two alternatives. One alternative is based on grades in selected English and math courses; the second alternative is based on SAT or ACT scores. See an advisor or check the current university catalog or course schedule book for clarification.

Core Curriculum: The general education requirements applied to all students entering the university as first-time college students or as transfers with fewer than 36 college credits. Copies of the Core can be obtained from the Office of Undergraduate Studies Advising Centers.

Dual Enrollment: A process by which students may enroll in courses at another college or university while maintaining their primary enrollment in another institution. Dual enrollment requires an advisor's approval and may not be used for certain Core and pre-major courses.

Forgiveness Policy: A procedure which allows a student to repeat a course and substitute the second grade for the first-attempt grade in calculating the grade point average. Both grades remain on the student's transcript. This policy may be used a maximum of three times in the undergraduate degree program.

Gordon Rule: A State of Florida policy which requires all students receiving a bachelor's degree to complete a minimum of 24,000 words of writing in designated courses and two mathematics courses, one of which must be Finite Math or higher at FIU. Gordon Rule courses require a grade of "C" or higher to be satisfactorily completed.

Grade Point Average (GPA): This represents an numerical analysis of the grades received in all courses completed within the university. The GPA is calculated for both the term and as a cumulative average for all courses in which grades are received.

Intended Majors: May be declared once a student has completed 30 credits and is in good academic standing. This is a process which allows a student to begin advising with a major department before becoming fully qualified for admission to the academic program.

Limited Access Programs: These majors have a competitive admissions process which generally requires higher standards for selection. Limited access programs may require a higher grade point average or some type of volunteer field experience or "hours," and may select students only once each year with a common starting date for all admits.

Majors: In order to declare a major, a student must meet all of the minimum requirements for admission to the program. This generally includes a minimum grade point average, completion of pre-major requirements, completion of the Core requirements, and completion of CLAST or an alternative.

Figure 1.1 Definition of Terms *(continued)*

Student Academic Advising System (SASS): An automated degree audit system, the SASS provides information regarding progress toward a degree. It includes information about which courses have been completed for the Core and for a specific major. The SASS report also provides information about whether or not other requirements are completed, including the summer course requirement, GPA, and CLAST.

Transfer Credits: Credits earned at another college or university, credits earned through AP or IB programs, and credits completed through dual enrollment are considered transfer credits and are applied to the total credits earned. These credits do not apply to the GPA or to credits attempted.

Warning, Probation and Dismissal: Three levels of warning regarding poor academic performance. *Warning* is the first level and occurs the first time a student's cumulative GPA drops below a 2.00. The second level, *probation,* occurs the second consecutive term that the cumulative GPA is below a 2.00. The final stage, *dismissal,* occurs the next term after probation when both the term and cumulative GPA fall below a 2.00. Dismissal is for one calendar year and requires an application for readmission.

Summary • • • • • • • • • • • • • • • • •

Are you feeling ready for college now? The next few weeks and months will be filled with surprises and even one or two shocks! The better you prepare yourself, the more successful you will be as a student. The more open you are to new people and new experiences, the more you will learn about yourself. This is the time to begin assuming responsibility for yourself in this new and sometimes challenging environment. Some of the "old" strategies from high school may work; many more will not.

Read everything; ask questions; understand consequences. The most successful students, in our experience, are those who quickly learn to take responsibility for themselves, use the vast resources available within the university, and become engaged in the exciting process of learning!

·················· **Exercise 1.1 Find Someone Who . . .** ··················

1. Was born under my astrological sign. _____

2. Likes Chinese food. _____

3. Reads novels for fun. _____

4. Was born in another state or country. Where? _____

5. Likes Madonna. _____

6. Plays a musical instrument. Which one? _____

7. Favorite color is green. _____

8. Has a part-time job. _____

9. Has his/her own car. _____

10. Sleeps in a water bed. _____

11. Has been to Europe. _____

12. Has been to a Marlins game. _____

13. Played a varsity sport in high school. _____

14. Lives or plans to live on campus. _____

15. Has blue eyes. _____

16. I've never met before. _____

17. Has a pet other than a dog or cat. What? _____

18. Has been scuba diving or snorkeling. _____

19. Has parachuted or bungee jumped. _____

20. Is registered to vote. _____

·········· **Exercise 1.2 Important Names and Numbers** ··········

Class	Instructor	Office Location	Phone
_____	_____	_____	_____
_____	_____	_____	_____
_____	_____	_____	_____
_____	_____	_____	_____
_____	_____	_____	_____

The more familiar you are with your campus, activities, and important dates, the more likely you will be successful and meet with as few roadblocks as possible.

Learning important information such as drop and add deadlines and where the Registrar's Office is located can help make things run smoother for you. Study the **Student Handbook,** the **Undergraduate Catalog,** and other materials you were given in Orientation and in this class. You will find this information just as valuable as that disseminated in your other classes.

The following exercise will assist you in learning just a few of the items that could be valuable aspects of your academic success.

1. You need to be advised by an academic advisor. You have 14 credits. Where do you go? (name of office and location)

2. You were wondering if FIU has childcare for your three-year-old. Do we?

3. When is the last day to return books to the bookstore for a full refund?

4. I have lost my keys. Where do I go to look for them?

5. I have always wanted to work for a radio station. Does FIU have one?

6. When does sorority or fraternity rush begin?

7. Ever since that one-night stand, I've been meaning to get an AIDS test. Does the Health and Wellness Center offer it?

8. I'm interested in attending Florida Marlins baseball games. Is there a place on campus to purchase tickets?

9. I have financial aid. When I register, will my schedule be automatically validated, or is there something I need to do?

10. If I want to put money on my ID card, do I go to the Cashier's Office in PC?

11. I heard that there are famous people who speak at FIU. Is this true?

12. I have to take the CLAST, and I heard there is a workshop I can attend to help me do better. Where do I go to sign up for that workshop?

13. I got a parking ticket for parking on the grass (there were no other spaces). How do I appeal my ticket?

14. What movie is showing this Friday?

15. I would like to write for the student newspaper. What is it called, and where do I go for more information?

16. I have a learning disability. Can someone on campus provide me with assistance?

17. I know all about the Golden Panther Express, but I would like to buy a MetroBus pass. Is there somewhere on campus where I can do that? If so, where?

18. I'm tired already. When is the next university holiday?

19. When is registration week for the next term?

20. How many times can an undergraduate student take advantage of the forgiveness policy?

21. How much is a round-trip ticket on the Golden Panther Express?

22. When is the next comedy show?

23. Name two restaurants/eateries on campus.

24. What is the name of the place where our men's and women's basketball teams play?

25. Does FIU have a swimming pool? If so, where?

CHAPTER 2

Answering Academic Questions

"Knowledge comes, but wisdom lingers."
—Alfred, Lord Tennyson

Attitude •

Why start a chapter on academics with a section on attitude? We thought about this for a long time before deciding to begin here. We know that effective students usually have a positive attitude about learning and that ineffective students usually have a negative attitude. The best students see every class session as an opportunity to learn something new, explore some concept in depth, or just challenge themselves to think. A positive attitude is not about getting grades; it is about the process of learning and growing. So "attitude" is a good place to start thinking about academics and all the small details you need to learn quickly.

Bored in this class? See it as useless? If so, that is **your** choice! Students who profess to be bored or disinterested in a class have made a choice and no amount of effort on our part or on the part of other students in this class will change things.

Take a minute or two to assess your attitude before moving on to the academic information provided in this chapter.

So, how is your attitude today? What did you learn about yourself? Is there anything you may want or need to change?

Academics: Why Are You Here? • • •

The information in this chapter is designed to help you make the kinds of decisions and choices you will face this term (and, perhaps, every term thereafter). Most of your choices, challenges, and successes will be directly or indirectly linked to your academic work; yet, many students know little or nothing about the details of academic life beyond what other students say to them.

This chapter will provide some general information about the various "systems" you will experience—advising, registration, grades. It will also suggest some "decisions" you will face—which courses to take, where to find information, and how to keep yourself on solid academic footing.

The Core Curriculum • • • • • • • • • • •

Let's begin with some information about the university curriculum. The curriculum is the course of study outlined by the university and its several colleges to educate students. A university's curriculum almost always includes a set of common or general requirements and a set of specific or concentrated requirements.

Figure 2.1 Attitude Checklist

✔	Positive	✔	Negative
	1. I am attending school because I want to be here. 2. I feel that advanced education will help me have a good life. 3. Going to school is worth the sacrifices I must make. 4. My school work gets top priority. 5. I never miss class without a good reason. 6. I want to learn all I can while I'm here. 7. When I'm interested in learning something, I often do more than the assigned work. 8. I believe most teachers are interested in helping me learn.		1. I do as little as I can to get by. 2. I'm here because I don't know what else I want to do. 3. I often wonder if advanced education is worth the financial investment. 4. I rarely see the relevance between my courses and what I want to do with my life. 5. I resent the time I have to spend studying. 6. Most teachers do as little as possible and don't really care if I learn anything. 7. I cut class whenever I think I can get away with it. 8. I expect to drop out before I graduate.

The general requirements begin in the freshman year and require that you complete a sequence of courses known as a "Core Curriculum" or "General Education." This sequence of courses is required for graduation, regardless of your academic major. For purposes of discussion, we'll use the term "Core" to describe these requirements although this terminology is not used at all universities. The Core is divided into several general categories within which are listed a number of specific course options used to fulfill the requirements.

Typical Core requirements generally include courses in English, mathematics, the natural sciences, humanities, the arts, and the social sciences. The categories under which specific courses are listed may have different names, but each course will fall into one of these disciplines. Students select specific courses to meet the required number of credits and distribution across the disciplines. In some categories, there will be a number of choices; in others, only a specific course may be used to meet the requirement.

The Core may also include required courses that are "interdisciplinary" and do not fit a specific discipline. The university, however, believes the course or courses are important for its students. This first-year experience course is a good example of an interdisciplinary course that provides the opportunity for you to explore a wide range of topics and issues central to your success as a student. Once completed, these Core courses provide at least an acquaintance with all of the major academic disciplines. You will have become, in theory, a well-rounded student prepared to face the rigors of specialization!

Regardless of where you attend college, this type of a requirement will have to be completed. Most colleges provide a list of the Core courses, as well as a list of courses which are required for certain majors. These course lists should become a part of your permanent file and be used each term to check off which are completed.

Generally, all Core requirements are completed in the first two years of college. Some students, however, may not complete everything until the end of the junior year because of their planned academic major and its pre-major requirements.

Pre-Major Requirements • • • • • • • •

In addition to the Core Curriculum, you will also complete required courses for your intended major. Some majors have several requirements, some of which will be included in the Core requirements; other majors have no prerequisite courses.

Pre-requisite courses, unlike "Core" courses, usually relate in some way to your planned major. Some courses may be used to fulfill both Core and pre-major requirements. It is a good idea to become familiar with which courses are required for any of the possible majors that interest you. Select courses that, to the extent possible, complete both "Core" **and** pre-major requirements. You'll save time and money!

Students who are undecided about a major or who change their intended major may have to complete additional pre-requisite courses before applying to their major department. Some academic programs will expect that admitted students have completed all pre-requisites as well as the Core; other majors are more flexible in admitting students.

Responsibility • • • • • • • • • • • • • • • • •

Does all of this sound confusing? It probably is! What is important to remember is that you, the student, now assume responsibility for your education. To this point in your academic life, someone else has been watching out for you and monitoring which courses you took—a guidance counselor, your parents, a teacher in your high school. No one will assume this role for you in college; you are the person who is "in charge" of your educational experiences in and outside the classroom.

The university assumes you have read everything sent to you and that you understand all of it. Further, if you don't understand, it is assumed you will ask questions. Using Exercise 2.1, let's assess your "Responsibility Quotient" (RQ) at this point in your academic career.

How did you do? If you scored well, you are probably looking out for your interests and will continue to build your skills as an informed student. If your score was low, ask yourself why. What do you need to change?

Academic Advising • • • • • • • • • • • • •

In most universities, first-year students receive their academic advising from an undergraduate Academic Advising Center which may be separate unit or a part of a college. Advising centers offer both individual and group advising for students. Conducted by a trained faculty or staff member, these advising sessions provide you with an opportunity to ask questions,

identify courses for the next term, and discuss your intended major plans.

Before you go to see an advisor, think about how you want to use the time. A good starting point is to list all of the general questions you have. Then consider specific questions about which classes to take and what requirements you need to fulfill. Use the following guide to assist you in preparing for your advising session.

Figure 2.2 Advising Guide

In my first term, I will meet with my advisor and:

1. Review by AP, CLEP, or IB credits, if any.
2. Review my placement test scores.
3. Review the Core requirements.
4. Review my intended major requirements, if any.
5. Select my next term's courses.
6. Discuss any problems I'm having in courses.
7. Learn how to add and drop a class.

In my second term, I will learn from my advisor about:

1. How to declare an intended major.
2. How and when to register for CLAST.
3. Which courses to take in the next term.
4. How to read a SASS report.
5. Making any necessary adjustments to my SASS report.

Do any of these questions require an immediate answer? If so, you may want to visit the Advising Center fairly soon. Advisors are always interested in talking with students, whether it is time for formal advising or just to answer a quick question.

The Class Schedule • • • • • • • • • • • •

Each term a university prepares a class schedule that lists all of the courses to be taught that term. General information including important telephone numbers, registration directions, and an academic calendar with key dates may be included along with specific information about classes to be taught, including days and times, registration reference numbers, and names of assigned professors.

Class schedule information may appear in any of several formats including a printed booklet or a section of the university's web page. Web schedules are usually up-to-date and immediately reflect all additions and changes made. For this reason, most large universities are eliminating the printed booklet in favor of an up-to-date online system.

Students need to learn to access the university's registration system, including the online class schedule, in order to register for classes. Access is available through a personal computer at home with an Internet connection or through on-campus computers available in labs and the library. Also, campuses often have registration access through computer "kiosks" located in various academic buildings and student centers. In addition to registration, students may access other information including grades, unofficial transcripts, and information about "holds" that might prevent future registration. Knowing how to access and use the registration system is a vital tool for students.

In many universities, students are advised before the term class schedule is available. It is a good idea, therefore, to select several alternative courses when you meet with your advisor. Not every course for which you want or need to register is offered every term!

Advising Holds • • • • • • • • • • • • • •

An advising hold is placed on students to assure that an advisor is seen. While not all Advising Centers do this, many find that it is a useful way to assure that all or certain groups of students are receiving some assistance in negotiating the academic system. In addition, some academic departments, schools, and colleges place advising holds on their students to assure that proper advising occurs once the major is declared.

An advising hold will prevent you from registering if you have not seen your advisor. While students often know which classes they want to take, they generally benefit from spending time with a skilled advisor or faculty member who knows the university's academic programs. A hold is there to help you avoid some of the common pitfalls in course selection.

Pitfalls? What pitfalls? Common ones include registering for a class that is too advanced or has certain prerequisites you've not yet completed. Some students select the wrong class because the title **sounds the same as** a required course. While an advisor will

rarely assist you with the process of registering, she can help you save some time, effort, and, once again, even save you some money by checking over the courses you plan to take!

Registration • • • • • • • • • • • • • • • • •

Students eligible to register for classes are usually assigned a specific registration day and time based on the number of credits attempted or earned to date. Some universities give registration preference to seniors; others give preference to freshmen.

How students register for classes depends on what type of registration system is in place. The three most common systems are registration in person; registration by telephone; and, registration by computer. Let's briefly examine the strengths and weaknesses of each system.

Registering in Person • • • • • • • • • •

This is the most traditional method of registration and usually involves standing in line! The student presents a list of requested courses with specific days and times. These are entered into a computer to check for availability. If there is a seat in the requested class, the student is registered; if there is no seat, the student must immediately present an alternative selection.

Once the classes are selected, a schedule and bill are printed and provided to the student who then completes the registration process by making payment.

Registering by Telephone • • • • • • •

This method of registration allows students to connect by telephone directly with the university computer system to select classes. Using voice prompts, the telephone system asks the student a series of questions including specific information about course selection. If seats are available, the student is placed in the requested course and, once the entire schedule is selected, the students enters a code to complete the registration process. It is useful to have several alternate course days and times in mind as the course or section you select may be closed. It is likely, however, that other sections or courses are still open.

Students who register by telephone should visit the campus to pick up a printed copy of the schedule and bill. It is important to verify the accuracy of the schedule, as it is possible to incorrectly enter a reference number or grade option when registering by telephone. Remember the section on responsibility? Here is a good place to begin!

Telephone registration systems are now giving way to a better technology, the Web!

Computer or Web Registration •••

Most registration systems now make use of personal computers and the World Wide Web. From any personal computer with a modem, a student with an access code number can dial into the university computer, select courses, and register for them. An advantage to Web registration is that it provides visual feedback on the schedule (unlike the telephone system) and provides a list of alternative course sections if the selected section is not available.

An advantage to Web registration is that a schedule can be printed immediately on any printer linked to the personal computer. The system also provides a fee statement or bill at the same time.

A disadvantage is that not all students have personal computers. However, university computer labs can provide access to the Web and registration.

Closed Classes •••••••••••••••••

Once a course section is closed, no additional students may register for it. Permission to enroll can be given by the academic department or the individual instructor. This form of permission to register for a closed section is usually called an "override." Some professors gladly give overrides because they know a number of registered students will drop the class; other professors never give overrides because they feel their classes are already too full. Increasingly, seating capacity in classrooms determines whether or not a student may add a specific class.

If you are not able to register for a course you really want to take, sometimes it helps to attend the first class session and talk with the professor. Often professors allow students who are present that day to, in effect, take the seats of those registered students who are absent. Many high-demand classes are listed in the schedule with the notation "attendance required at the first class session." This means if you fail to attend, your seat will be given to another student.

Dropping or Adding Classes ••••••

Deadlines for dropping and adding classes are published in the university's academic calendar that appears in a number of publications including **University Catalog**, the **Student Handbook**, and the **Registration Web Page**. These deadlines are firm so it is a good idea to write them down and highlight them in your daily/weekly planning calendar.

Most universities allow students to freely drop and add classes for a specified period of time, usually the first week of the term. After the first week, a student has usually missed too much work to easily make it up. Better to wait another term to take the class than to start out at an academic disadvantage.

If you change your mind about certain classes and want to drop one or more after the first week, you must process a drop form in the Registrar's Office or through the online registration system. Failure to attend a class does not result in an automatic drop in most universities. It is always the student's responsibility (that word, again!) to know the specific procedures, deadlines, and forms for dropping a class. Talk with an advisor or your course instructor for this course if you have questions about dropping or adding courses.

Finding a Major •••••••••••••••

Many students believe they have declared their major at the time of admission to the university. You were probably asked to identify a major in your application for admission. This, however, is not binding for you or the university. This is called an "Intended Major." In fact, many new students are undecided about their major although they may have one or two ideas in mind.

After successfully completing a specific number of college credits, usually 25 to 40, a student may declare an **INTENDED MAJOR**. The "intended major" means that the student will receive advising from the selected academic department. Declaring an intended major is different from declaring a major.

In most universities, a student cannot **DECLARE A MAJOR** without meeting certain minimum requirements. These requirements often include:

1. Having a satisfactory GPA (usually 2.00 or higher).
2. Completing all the pre-major courses.
3. Completing a minimum number of credit hours.
4. Completing any required skills or competency tests.

In addition, some academic majors are identified as **LIMITED ACCESS PROGRAMS.** These programs have higher admission standards and are usually quite competitive. That is, not all students who apply will be admitted.

Many students declare an "intended major" at the end of their freshman year and then officially declare their major at the end of their sophomore year. Some students elect to wait until the end of their Sophomore year to make any formal decision about declaring a major.

The University Catalog • • • • • • • • •

The **University Catalog** provides a detailed explanation of all university policies and procedures. It is one of the best sources of information about academic programs and requirements, general academic policies, and names/degrees of the faculty. The catalog also provides information about the university's history, accreditation, and support services.

In the catalog, there is a detailed explanation of the university's grading system. Most universities use a 4.00 grading scale and may or may not award points for pluses and minuses. The grade point average (GPA) is presented in two parts, the first of which is based on courses taken in a specific term. This is called the **term GPA.** It is calculated by dividing the earned credits into the number of "points" generated by each grade. For example, let's assume a student has taken 15 credits and received the following grades where there is a 4.00 scale with pluses and minuses receiving differential points:

Course	Credits	Grade	Points
ENC 1101	3	B+	9.99 (3.33 x 3)
MAC 2132	3	C+	6.99 (2.33 x 3)
SPN 1120	5	A	20.00 (4.00 x 5)
SLS 1501	1	A	4.00 (1.00 x 4)
PSY 2020	3	C	6.00 (2.00 x 3)

Total Points = *46.98* ÷ 15 = 3.132

As this example shows, a strong grade in a course offered for more credit hours will help your GPA. A one-credit "A" is nice but it does not add much to the GPA. On the other hand, a five-credit "A" can be very helpful.

The **cumulative** or **institutional GPA** is the average for all credits taken and grades received. Classes from which you drop or withdraw are not counted in your GPA. The cumulative GPA is the one that is most important because it represents the summary of all of your course work to date. It is also the GPA that is used to determine your overall academic standing.

Academic Standing • • • • • • • • • • • •

There is "good news" and there is "bad news" when considering academic standing. On the extreme "bad news" side, if your cumulative GPA is below a 2.00, you'll probably be placed on an academic probation or perhaps be dismissed from the university. Different universities use different sanctions for dealing with poor academic performance. One frequently used system includes three tiers: warning, probation, and dismissal.

Under this model, the first term that your cumulative GPA falls below a 2.00, you are placed on **ACADEMIC WARNING.** The next term, if your cumulative GPA remains below a 2.00, you move to **ACADEMIC PROBATION.** If academic performance remains below a 2.0 for a third term, you are **DISMISSED** from the university.

A dismissal for academic reasons is usually for a minimum of one calendar year during which time you may not enroll in any classes. All warnings, probations, and dismissals are noted on your permanent academic transcript.

On the positive side, most universities reward students who are enrolled full-time in a given term and receive a 3.50 or higher. These students are placed on the **DEAN'S LIST** for that term. At graduation, students with a cumulative grade point average of 3.90 or higher graduate **SUMMA CUM LAUDE.** Those with a 3.70 to 3.899 graduate **MAGNA CUM LAUDE** and those with a cumulative GPA of 3.50 to 3.699 graduate **CUM LAUDE.**

These academic honors are based only on the university grade point average and do not include course work completed at other universities or through alternative methods like Advanced Placement. Designations of these academic honors appear on your permanent transcript and are listed in the Graduation Program.

Figure 2.3 Course Planning Guide

It is helpful to plan your class schedule several terms in advance. This allows you to think about courses in sequence, including Core requirements, pre-major (and major) requirements, and electives.

YEAR 1

Fall, 20_____   Spring, 20_____   Summer, 20_____

_____   _____   _____

_____   _____   _____

_____   _____   _____

_____   _____   _____

_____   _____   _____

_____   _____   _____

YEAR 2

Fall, _____   Spring, _____   Summer, _____

_____   _____   _____

_____   _____   _____

_____   _____   _____

_____   _____   _____

_____   _____   _____

_____   _____   _____

YEAR 3

Fall, _____   Spring, _____   Summer, _____

_____   _____   _____

_____   _____   _____

_____   _____   _____

_____   _____   _____

_____   _____   _____

_____   _____   _____

Advanced Placement, IB Credit, Placement Tests, and CLEP ••••••

There are several ways a student may earn credits before starting college. Some standardized examination scores may be used to fulfill core or pre-major requirements. The most frequently used alternatives are the Advanced Placement program (AP), the International Baccalaureate degree (IB), the College Level Examination Program (CLEP), and the SAT II Subject Examinations.

The **AP Program** requires that students complete certain designated courses in high school and take the appropriate subject examination. AP scores are submitted to the university which then determines the amount and type of credit to be awarded. AP scores and credits appear on the student's official transcript and often fulfill basic requirements for general education courses.

The **IB Degree**, like AP credit, requires that the student complete a specific course of study and take the appropriate subject examinations. Scores are awarded at the "Higher Level" and the "Lower Level." University credit is given based on the subject and the score submitted. No more than 30 credits may be awarded. IB credits may also be used to fulfill certain general education requirements.

CLEP is a testing program originally designed to award credits for study and learning outside the formal classroom. Older students who have worked, served in the military, or have other life experiences between high school and college most often use it. CLEP credits are granted in a number of subject areas and are based on the test scores submitted. CLEP tests may be taken at the local community colleges or other designated testing sites. A fee is required for each CLEP exam.

Placement Tests are given by the university and include tests for proficiency in reading, math, and writing. Scores are used to place students in the appropriate university course level and/or exempt them from certain courses or requirements. Placement tests are frequently given at orientation programs and at other designated times.

Academic Misconduct • • • • • • • • •

If rumors are to be believed, many students commit some form of academic misconduct during their college years. Sometimes it happens through ignorance on the student's part; other times, it is intentional. While some forms of academic misconduct are open to debate, other forms are clear and not open to interpretation.

In all cases, it is the student's responsibility to know the university's rules about academic misconduct and become informed about the potential consequences. A student involved in some form of academic misconduct may be given a failing grade in class, may be placed on some type of probation, may be suspended from the university for a fixed period of time, or may be permanently dismissed. Dismissal and suspension are noted on the student's permanent academic record.

While grades are important, cheating or plagiarism (using someone else's work as if it were your own) are not substitutes for study and preparation. Being unprepared for a test is never a good reason to cheat. Most professors explain early in the term how they handle academic misconduct in their classes. They may even include this information in their course syllabus. They will not, however, explain the university

policies and procedures in detail. These polices and procedures are published in the **University Catalog** or in the **Student Handbook.** Read them!

What are some of the common forms of academic misconduct? Let's complete Exercise 2.2 and see what you know!

Avoiding Academic Problems • • • •

Here are some guidelines which may help you avoid problems down the road:

1. Know the university policies and procedures. Ignorance of the rules is no excuse if you violate one of them.
2. Establish clear boundaries when working with other students on a project or assignment. Don't help others who want to cheat. Students who assist others to cheat are often held equally responsible.
3. Learn to manage your time and keep up with assignments. Students who cheat often panic when confronted with a test or an assignment for which they are not prepared.
4. Get help if it is difficult to keep up with assignments. Talk with the professor or a tutor; don't wait until the last minute to seek assistance.
5. Consult with an academic advisor. Sometimes it is necessary to drop a class in order to keep up. Know the deadline for dropping classes without penalty.
6. Set realistic goals and don't feel pressured by others, including family and friends.

Finding Academic Information • • •

Three primary sources of information about academics are the **University Catalog** and the **Student Handbook** which are published annually and the **University Web Page** that is updated frequently. Most academic questions can be answered by carefully reviewing these three important publications.

Faculty and academic advisors are also useful resources. If you are interested in a major, meet with a faculty member to discuss requirements for admission and career possibilities. Talk with an academic advisor about campus resources to assist you in exploring possible majors.

The **Student Handbook** is a quick reference to campus life. This publication includes policy and procedure resources like the student conduct code and the policy on academic misconduct. It also includes much information about support services and resources.

The **Student Handbook** and the **University Catalog** are two basic university resources for your bookshelf.

Summary • • • • • • • • • • • • • • • •

College is an exciting voyage of discovery. It will require that you challenge yourself as a student and, perhaps, as a person. If it is done right, your university experiences will provide you with life-long friendships, a genuine curiosity about the learning process, and a deeper understanding of yourself as a person.

Create an "attitude" about learning as much as you can and make use of all the academic resources available as you continue on your journey!

Figure 2.4 Top Ten List: Questions about Advising

10. Who is my advisor?
 9. Where is my advisor?
 8. What requirements do I need for my major?
 7. What "Core" requirements do I need to complete?
 6. Are my transfer/AP/dual enrollment credits on file and applied?
 5. Can I take courses at other universities and still be earning a degree here?
 4. How do I select a major?
 3. What can I do if I don't have a major in mind?
 2. When can I register?
 1. How do I tell my parents that I don't want to be a *(fill in the blank)?*

·············· **Exercise 2.1 Responsibility Quotient** ················

Using the following scale, assess your Responsibility Quotient (RQ) as a beginning student.

　　1 = No, I have not done this.

　　2 = Maybe I have done a little in this area.

　　3 = Yes, I have done this.

_____　　1.　I have read the **University Catalog.**

_____　　2.　I have read the **Student Handbook.**

_____　　3.　I know the prerequisites for my intended major.

_____　　4.　I have been to the university library and learned where basic resources are located.

_____　　5.　I bought all of my textbooks.

_____　　6.　I know the term deadline for dropping classes without academic penalty.

_____　　7.　I know where the health center and counseling center are located.

_____　　8.　I know the names of all my professors.

_____　　9.　I know where to go for academic advising.

_____　　10.　I know at least one person in each class and could call them for help if I missed class.

RQ Scoring Key

　　0–15 points　　How long do you plan to be here?

　　16–22 points　　A beginning, but there are more "basics" you need to earn.

　　23–30 points　　You're off to a great start . . . keep it up!

·············· Exercise 2.2 Walking the Academic Line ··············

Many students find themselves in difficulty because they never learned the "rules" about what is acceptable and what is not acceptable in completing academic assignments. Do you know where the academic "line" is drawn? Is the line always clear? Where would *you* draw the line?

Each of the following statements represents a situation you might face at some time in your college career. Ask yourself, "Would I do this? Are there possible consequences if I do this?"

1. Turning in a paper that someone else wrote for you.

2. Getting the answers to exam questions from someone in another section of the course.

3. Buying a paper from someone or taking one off of the Internet.

4. Asking a friend to proofread a paper and comment on it.

5. Working on a project or assignment with two or three other students.

6. Using the same paper to fulfill an assignment in two different classes.

7. Discussing with a classmate the types of questions that might be on a test.

8. Copying sections of a book or article and including them in your paper.

9. Having someone else take a test for you in a large lecture class where attendance is not taken.

10. Not reading the articles or books you include in a bibliography for a paper.

11. Using someone else's notes to write a paper.

12. Changing lab results when they do not turn out correctly.

13. Making up information for a paper because you did not have time to conduct the required interviews.

14. Making up journal entries for a class because you did not keep up with the assigned entries.

15. Using old exams from a club file to study for your test to be given by the same professor.

CHAPTER 3

Developing Relationships

*"Never doubt that a small group of committed
individuals can change the world; indeed,
that is the only thing that ever has."*
—Margaret Mead

Developing Relationships ･･･････

Going to college is perhaps the most difficult step that you have ever taken. It is difficult because of the many changes which will occur simultaneously in your life. Relationships will change too. You will change and others close to you will change.

There are reasons why change comes at this time in your life. First, there is a big difference between "going to school" and "attending college." It may immediately appear that there are no differences because you may be doing things in the same ways you did in high school: getting up, driving to school, going to classes, driving home, studying, and doing homework.

You will quickly discover, however, that university classes are probably larger than those you attended in high school. Some lecture sections may have as many as 200 students in class; this means the professor may not provide the same time and attention to you as a student. Some may not even know your name. You may know some people in your class or you may see no familiar faces. Further, no one but you will monitor what you do in and out of class. **You** will decide whether to attend or not. **You** will decide whether or not to buy your textbooks. **You** will decide whether or not to complete assignments and turn them in on time.

This new independence is difficult for some students who find the added responsibilities too challenging. In high school, others watched out for you; in the university, you watch out for yourself. As you begin to explore your new freedoms and choices, you are likely to make some good decisions and some poor decisions. Important relationships in your life will begin to change as you learn to handle each situation.

You will meet people who do not view the world in the same ways you and your family do. Some of these people will be students and some will be professors. You will make choices about your openness to new experiences and new people. If college is about learning, it includes what we learn from others about ourselves, our values, and our beliefs.

In this chapter, we will explore some of the ways in which your relationships with others will change during your time in college. We will also consider questions of difference and openness to change.

Living with Parents ･･･････････

New college students who continue to live at home almost immediately find a change in various long-standing relationships in their lives. As students begin to assert a new-found independence, many find that relationships with parents become strained. For students, the freshman year is a time for meeting new people, developing new ways of managing day-to-day decisions, and becoming more independent in the choices made. It is a rite into adulthood. For parents, this first year of college is a time to let go and establish new relationships with you as a young adult.

The problem is, however, that some parents have difficulty letting go. The problem is magnified when you continue to live at home. Parents often assume that you will keep the same hours as you maintained in high school, be available for family-related activities, and continue to perform certain household chores or manage family responsibilities. They may not realize that students really do study in the library past midnight, attend events on campus that don't begin until 10:00 p.m., and have classes that begin or end at unusual times.

You probably want your parents to be there to listen, but not tell you what to do. Your parents may say they want you to be independent but then don't seem to trust your judgment when you make your own decisions. What is needed is compromise on both sides. Be patient and allow your parents to adapt to the changes you are making and the new demands placed on your time. They are not being difficult; they are just accustomed to the way things have been at home for many years.

How are your relationships at home right now? Over the years, most students have developed a level of trust with their parents. As you have grown and matured, the trust and corollary freedoms given to you have increased. Open and honest discussion with your parents before you encounter problems is a good way to begin exploring what changes may be needed now that you are in college. Anger and confrontation create hostilities on both sides and rarely lead to any productive changes for either of you.

Remember that your adjustment to college and its demands, if you continue to live at home, is almost as difficult for your parents as it is for you. They are beginning to realize that you are finally a "grown-up" and that you have begun the process of leaving home for good. Subconsciously, they know that in just a few years, you will graduate, join the professional working world, and be on your own with your own family and responsibilities!

Living on Campus • • • • • • • • • • • • •

Most college campuses provide some type of on-campus residence halls or apartments for students who either live too far away to commute from home or who want the experience of living away from home. Living on campus provides more freedom and independence but also carries more responsibility; for some students, it proves to be more difficult than living at home. Every year, there are students who move into college residence halls and do not make it through the first night without calling home or, in some cases, returning home without ever attending a class!

Living on campus can be an exciting, challenging experience which provides many opportunities to learn about living on your own within a supportive environment. Roommates, resident assistants, other students, and professional staff can provide assistance and encouragement as you make the transition to college. There are people with whom you can talk about what you're experiencing. Better still, there are other students who share some of the same experiences and feelings.

For many students the biggest change from home to campus living is learning to live with others. At home, relationships were established over many years of living together. Once you move into a residence hall, you have to start developing a new set of relationships, often with people who are total strangers. Living with another person presents wonderful opportunities and, sometimes, presents serious problems.

Don't wait for little problems to reach crisis proportions! As soon as possible, sit and talk with your roommate about each other's idiosyncrasies. In a living situation, compromise is essential. If you are a night owl and your roommate likes to go to sleep right after the 11 o'clock news, you need to discuss how the two of you can compromise so that you don't argue every night about one another's habits.

There are many possible points of conflict that you can anticipate and discuss up front such as cleanliness, sharing cleaning duties, taking phone messages, having overnight guests, and adhering to university

and housing rules and regulations. You will find that if you discuss differences, you can head off many potential problems. You can also find ways to compromise so that each of you feels "at home" and can maintain your preferred personal and academic routines. Keep in mind that early discussions are more likely to resolve issues than waiting until there is a problem and you or your roommate is angry.

Should you find that all your efforts fail and that you just can't get along with your roommate, don't allow the situation to have a negative affect on your academics. Make an appointment with a housing staff member to discuss the problem and what attempts have been made to alleviate the situation. You will receive advice as to what to do next, including a possible move to another room. Leaving college or moving back home should be a last resort! Learning to cope with others different from you is part of your education and will be invaluable in your future endeavors.

Living on campus can be a rewarding experience and will allow you to continue your growth and maturation to independent adulthood. While it is not always easy to live in a college residence hall, students who have this experience often form friendships that last for the rest of their lives.

Having A Boyfriend/Girlfriend ••••

Just when you think everything is going well—you made an "A" on your first college examination, you got a raise at work, and you won a pair of free tickets to a sold-out concert—you get a phone call from your boyfriend or girlfriend telling you that he/she wants to break up with you. Your world suddenly comes crashing down.

There is never a good time for a break-up, but during college, broken relationships often have a negative impact on academics. A relationship takes time, energy, and commitment, all of which are also required to be a successful student. Losing an important relationship can send you into a downspin that, if you are not careful, may cause you to hit bottom. Grades may drop and you may feel overwhelmed by all of the pressures.

The same recommendations suggested for dealing with roommates are useful in relationship problems. You should discuss the possible effects that college attendance may have on your relationship even if you have been dating for a long time and feel you know one another very well. If attending the same university, or living in the same town, share your class schedules and the amount of time you each may need for studying. Add time for extra-curricular activities, work, and other time commitments that may not involve time together. Your relationship doesn't have to suffer if you plan ahead and are clear with regard to your expectations.

The situation changes if your boyfriend/girlfriend lives elsewhere. The relationship may become strained simply because of distance. You will each meet new people and develop lives apart from one another. Be prepared for this potential problem and openly discuss your expectations. Is it okay to go out with other people? How often will you try to see one another? Talk on the telephone? Send e-mail or write letters?

Regardless of what your personal situation is, a sour romance can really put you down in the dumps. Believe it or not, it will pass! As the old song says, "breaking up is hard to do," but you will get over it. College is one of the best places to meet new people if you are interested. You can strike up a conversation with someone in class, in the library, or in the cafeteria; you can join a club or play intramural sports. From there, you are on your own!

If things are not going well, don't hurt in silence. Talk to a friend or relative; make an appointment with the university counseling center to speak with a staff member. It is perfectly normal to discuss your problems with another person, whether it is a friend or a staff member who is professionally educated to work with students. If you do decide to talk with a counseling center staff member, all conversations are confidential.

During the coming years, you will form a number of relationships and friendships. Some will be more serious than others; some will develop into life-long friendships, while others will fade away. One of these relationships may even develop into the "love" of your life! You will face challenges, particularly in your first year of college when you are feeling most alone and are, perhaps, separated from your family and friends. Learn from the challenges; use the campus resources available to assist you as you gain new experiences.

Differences Are Valuable ••••••••

A college or university campus is one of the few places where every facet of society can be found, and every conflicting voice has a right to be heard. There may be times when you will be offended by what you see or hear on campus; realize that these occasions, too, are a part of your education! While you may not agree with or condone what others do or say, it is an opportunity for you to understand others better. On campus, open dialogue and discussion of issues is important to the academic process known as "academic freedom."

In the classroom, faculty members have the right to present materials and differing points of view and to delve into controversial areas openly and honestly. You will sometimes find a class uncomfortable because the views presented are different from your own; you may even feel that the professor has crossed the boundary of good taste or is talking about matters not appropriate to a college classroom. When you find yourself in this situation, ask yourself what is happening. Are your beliefs being challenged? Is the topic one that is never discussed at home?

In fact, if your education is to be genuinely valuable to you, you should encounter differing views; you should feel a little uncomfortable. More important, you should be open to hearing what professors and other students have to say! Be open to learning from others and you will learn a lot. You may not change your values or beliefs but you will have consciously chosen them from among a range of options.

Non-Traditional Students • • • • • • •

Most of the students in this class are recent high school graduates who are considered "traditional" college students. In fact, many students are older when they begin college. Some have worked or served in the military; others have been raising children or have retired from their job; some are single parents; some are in school "just for the fun of it!" Many are attending college part-time while they hold full-time jobs or balance home and family responsibilities; some attend classes only at night or on the weekends. These are considered "non-traditional" students. They make up a growing segment of every university campus today.

As you sit in your classes, look around and see if there are any non-traditional students. Older students often have knowledge and expertise that can be valuable in and outside the classroom; yet, traditional students are often reluctant to approach them. It is difficult to return to college or begin college after a long absence from a classroom; don't be afraid to introduce yourself to a non-traditional student. Invite him or her to participate in a study group or to join you for coffee after class.

Students with Disabilities • • • • • • • •

Another growing population on college campuses is students with disabilities. While some are visible, many more are invisible because of the nature of the disability. Many students come to campus with little knowledge of the various disabilities and little experience in dealing with a person who is disabled in some way.

The most visible of the disabilities are those which are physical: the student in a wheelchair; the student using a guide dog or a cane; the student wearing a hearing aid. Many other students, however, have some form of learning disability that may not be apparent to the casual observer. On the first day of class, for example, a professor may ask for volunteer note takers to assist one or more students whose disability makes note taking difficult. You could volunteer and, as a result, become acquainted with a student who requires some accommodation in order to meet course requirements. This will broaden your experience and provide assistance to another student.

Most campuses have offices that provide assistance to students with disabilities to assure that the campus and all of its programs and services are accessible, regardless of the accommodation required. Under requirements of the Americans with Disabilities Act, any student should be able to participate in any activity or academic program offered to all students. Over the years, campuses have modified their buildings to include ramps, elevators, visual as well as audio fire alarms, and wheelchair seating in athletic arenas and theaters. Access on campus has made it possible for more students with disabilities to attend their college of choice and to successfully complete their degree of choice.

Race and Ethnicity • • • • • • • • • • •

Race and ethnic background are among the most common differences on a college campus. For many students, college is the first place they will meet people who are different from themselves in ways that are very apparent to the casual observer. Race is one of these differences and ethnic or cultural background is another.

You will probably meet people from other countries who have come to the campus to study; you will also meet people from other parts of this country whose backgrounds are different from your own. Each person you meet who is culturally or racially different from you presents an opportunity to learn about another culture or their race. In addition, the campus offers many opportunities to learn about other cultures through clubs and organizations, through programs and social activities, and through formal classes for which you might register.

Sexual Orientation ••••••••••••

Another visible population on many campuses are gay, lesbian, and bisexual students. College is a place where many students openly explore and question their sexual identity or orientation. It is generally accepted that approximately 10 percent of the general population is gay or lesbian, so it is likely you already know someone who is gay. Consider this as another opportunity to expand your appreciation for differences.

For many students, college is the place where they discover they are sexually attracted to someone of the same sex. Some students have been aware of such feelings for years but have never acted on them. These feelings may be unsettling because they are often in direct conflict with family beliefs, religious teachings, and attitudes of friends. To admit one might be gay or lesbian may mean being rejected by family or friends. Worse yet, it might mean being subjected to verbal harassment or physical attack.

Other students who are not gay may learn for the first time that a good friend or family member is lesbian or gay. This, too, can be unsettling and challenge one's beliefs. What does it mean if my friend is gay? How will others perceive me? How will I feel about that? What if a parent or sibling "comes out?" What will this mean to the family's relationships? These are difficult questions for which there are no simple answers.

There are many resources available to assist students who are dealing with questions of sexual orientation, whether it is their own or someone close to them. Gay and lesbian student organizations exist on many campuses; counseling centers have trained staff to provide assistance. Some campuses offer gay/lesbian studies or gender studies courses that provide an academic perspective on sexual orientation. Students who are harassed may use services available under the campus sexual harassment policy or other non-discrimination policies.

The biggest question for you is knowing who you are, understanding and accepting your feelings, and being open to others who may hold different views. You don't have to agree with someone's personal choices to be caring and supportive as a friend.

Understanding Diversity ••••••••

Most students do not consider diversity on a day-to-day basis. Some simply are unaware; others have limited contact with certain groups, have no friends who are different from them, and see no reason to make changes in friendship patterns or relationships. Let's consider a context in which the importance of awareness and broadening one's knowledge of others might become more important.

According to information published by the United Nations in an **Information Bulletin (December 1997)**, there are approximately 5.8 billion people in the world. Think about this population as it might be represented on a campus of 100 students. The campus population would include (based on world demographics) the following mix of students:

57 Asians
20 Europeans
7 North Americans
7 South Americans
9 Africans

Seventy percent of our group would be non-white and 30 percent white; 65 percent would be non-Christian and 35 percent would be Christian; 70 percent would not be able to read; 50 percent would suffer from malnutrition; 80 percent would live in substandard housing. The odds are only one would complete a university degree! Students in this university would know that half of the entire wealth in the world is controlled by six people, three from the United States, two from Japan, and one from Germany.

Is there a reason to become more aware of the diversity which exists around you? Keep this mythical university in mind because it represents the world in which you live and will work.

Let's go back for a moment and ask how all of this diversity is affecting **YOU**. To create new visions and missions, isn't it necessary for everyone to consider the impact of diversity at the individual and personal levels? If we are to become change agents and allies, don't we first have to become aware of our own inherent beliefs about others? And in the process, don't we also have to become aware of how these beliefs affect the day-to-day choices we make about our behavior?

Valuing diversity begins with understanding yourself. It means taking a closer look at your own experiences, background, and culture. What are the messages from your background that you embrace? That you feel might be hindering you in some way?

How do you view others? Are you aware of your own stereotypes and biases? How do you view others who are different from you?

Once you have faced the first challenge, AWARE-NESS, you are ready to continue exploring some additional concepts regarding diversity.

Stereotypes ••••••••••••••••••

John Glenn, the first man to orbit the earth (1962), participated in another space flight when he was 77 years old. Reactions were positive, for the most part, but gave rise to many questions. Should a 77-year-old man participate in a space flight even for scientific purposes? Is he crazy or just trying to recapture his youth? Could he manage the grueling physical, psychological, and emotional stress? Is this good for a person of his age? Are the skills and abilities required for this mission found in an older person?

Think about your reactions for a moment and be honest with yourself! What are the assumptions we often make about "older" people? Are they viewed as less productive? Less physically able? Slower? Not as able to learn new things? What John Glenn did by participating in a space flight at age 77, violates our **stereotypes** about older people.

Stereotypes are views and attitudes based on our assumptions about certain groups of people. These assumptions may or may not accurately represent the group but may guide our actions toward that group or our beliefs about that group. Let's consider another situation and look at how stereotypes might influence thinking.

You are at the library and see a pregnant woman checking out a number of books on parenting. What are your assumptions? You might make the assumption that she is pregnant for the first time and wants to learn all about parenting. Your brain has interpreted some limited information by using your past experiences and beliefs about what you have observed to make a decision about this woman. Your assumptions might even be correct.

What you do not know, however, is that the woman you observed has a younger brother who recently adopted a young child and became a single parent. She is checking out the books for him because she thinks he will find them useful. She found them useful when her first child was born.

Missing information changes your view of the situation, doesn't it? Now you might ask yourself about your stereotypes regarding single men who adopt children!

Some common forms of stereotyping include the following:

Abelism: A system of exclusion and discrimination that oppresses people who have mental, emotional, or physical disabilities.

Anti-Semitism: Systematic discrimination against, condemnation, or oppression of Jews, Judaism, and the cultural, intellectual, and religious heritage of the Jewish people.

Classism: Individual, institutional, and societal beliefs and practices that assign differential value to people according to their socio-economic class.

Heterosexism: Individual, institutional, and societal beliefs based on the assumption that heterosexuality is the only normal and acceptable sexual orientation.

Sexism: Individual, institutional, and societal beliefs and practices that privilege men, subordinate women, and denigrate values and practices associated with women.

Racism: The systematic subordination of members of targeted racial groups who have relatively little social power in this country. This subordination is supported by individual, institutional, and societal beliefs and practices.

What are your stereotypes? What views based on limited information have you formed about others? How did you acquire these views and attitudes? Have you encountered exceptions, that is individuals who do not fit the stereotype? The following exercise will help you in exploring your stereotypes.

Prejudice and Discrimination •••••

There are two more concepts which are important if you are to fully understand and begin to value differences. These are **prejudice** and **discrimination**.

Prejudice refers to a negative attitude toward members of some distinct group based solely on their membership in that group. Prejudice has behavioral, cognitive, and affective components. In other words, prejudice affects our choices, the way we see the world, the way we interpret information, and the way we feel. All of these components can cause one to take actions that may discriminate against others.

We learn prejudice just like we learn everything else: by hearing the views expressed by our parents, teachers, friends, and the media. In some cases, children are rewarded for adopting the views of their elders and punished in some way if they do not.

To begin combating prejudice, your own and that of others, the following steps are useful:

1. Become aware of your own prejudices and their origins.
2. Educate yourself about the customs and beliefs of other cultures and peoples.
3. Challenge others' prejudicial statements, ideas, and beliefs.
4. Increase contacts with individuals and groups you might otherwise avoid or with whom you might not interact on a regular basis.

Discrimination involves negative actions toward another person. Actions may be mild or severe. Avoidance, for example, is a mild form of discrimination. Not inviting someone of a different race, age, or with a disability to join a study group could be considered a form of discrimination. This form of discrimination is subtle and often denied by those who engage in it.

The most severe forms of discrimination include outward aggression and violence. Consider the pictures you've seen of the civil wars in Bosnia or in the Middle East that, in part, are linked to religious and ethnic differences among people in those regions. Consider the Civil Rights movement in this country during the 1960s or, more recently, the reports of attacks on people who are gay or lesbian. These, too, are examples of violence directed at one group by another group.

In order to combat stereotypes and discrimination, it is important to be open-minded, ask questions, and become a good listener. You need to confront your own feelings and attitudes, become better informed about people different from yourself, and challenge others who use stereotypes or discriminate in some way. Finally, become aware of media images and the possible biases presented, both positive and negative. A good way to begin is with your own campus environment.

Summary

The next time you come to class, look at the classmate sitting to your right and to your left. Look at the person seated in front and behind you. These classmates are experiencing similar problems in adjusting to college. They are questioning their old habits, beliefs, and attitudes. They, too, are meeting new people different from themselves and are learning more about themselves in relation to others.

How many of your classmates have you met? Have you elected to sit with someone you already know, perhaps a friend from high school? Have you introduced yourself to anyone who appears to be different from you in some way? Someone who is older? Of a different race? With a disability? New relationships and friendships are an important part of this exciting time in your life; welcome them as learning experiences that will expand your horizons, make you a better student, and better prepare you for the world of work. The first step is the most difficult; why not start with those four people seated near you?

······ **Exercise 3.1 Parent Relationships: An Assessment** ······

Relationships with parents or other individuals who have been involved in raising you can become difficult as you approach and enter college. This is a time during which both you and they are undergoing some major life changes. Let's take a few minutes to assess what has been happening and what you would like to see happen in the next few months.

Part I. My Current Situation

1. Right now, I am living:　　_____ at home with my parents and siblings.
　　　　　　　　　　　　　　_____ at home with one parent and siblings.
　　　　　　　　　　　　　　_____ on campus in a residence hall.
　　　　　　　　　　　　　　_____ in my own apartment or home.

2. There are other family members living in our house: _____yes _____no _____sometimes

3. I share a room with:　　_____ a brother or sister.
　　　　　　　　　　　　　　_____ another family member or spouse.
　　　　　　　　　　　　　　_____ a roommate in the residence hall.
　　　　　　　　　　　　　　_____ no one. I have my own room.

4. With regard to transportation to school:　_____ I have my own car.
　　　　　　　　　　　　　　　　　　　　　　_____ I drive a car my parents own.
　　　　　　　　　　　　　　　　　　　　　　_____ I share a car with a sibling.
　　　　　　　　　　　　　　　　　　　　　　_____ I use public transportation.
　　　　　　　　　　　　　　　　　　　　　　_____ I live on campus and have no car.

5. Most of my school expenses are paid by:　_____ me.
　　　　　　　　　　　　　　　　　　　　　　_____ my parents.
　　　　　　　　　　　　　　　　　　　　　　_____ financial aid.
　　　　　　　　　　　　　　　　　　　　　　_____ a combination.

6. For spending money, I:　_____ have a part-time job.
　　　　　　　　　　　　　　_____ have a full-time job.
　　　　　　　　　　　　　　_____ use savings.
　　　　　　　　　　　　　　_____ get money from parents or relatives.

7. In my living situation:　_____ I decide when I come and go.
　　　　　　　　　　　　　　_____ There are some rules I have to follow.
　　　　　　　　　　　　　　_____ We discuss what I can and can't do.
　　　　　　　　　　　　　　_____ Rules are very restrictive for me.

8. I am the: _____oldest child _____middle child _____youngest child

9. I am the first child in my family to go to college. _____yes _____no

Summary Statement: In my living situation, I feel . . .

Part II. Thinking About My Relationship with Parents

As you think about your living situation and your family, what thoughts do you have about yourself and your relationships with parents and siblings or other family members?

1. As I thought about my living situation, I became aware that . . .

2. My parents sometimes surprise me when they . . .

3. I wish my parents understood about . . .

4. If I could say anything to my parents right now it would be . . .

Summary Statement: I see my relationships at home as . . .

Exercise 3.2 Cultural Pursuit

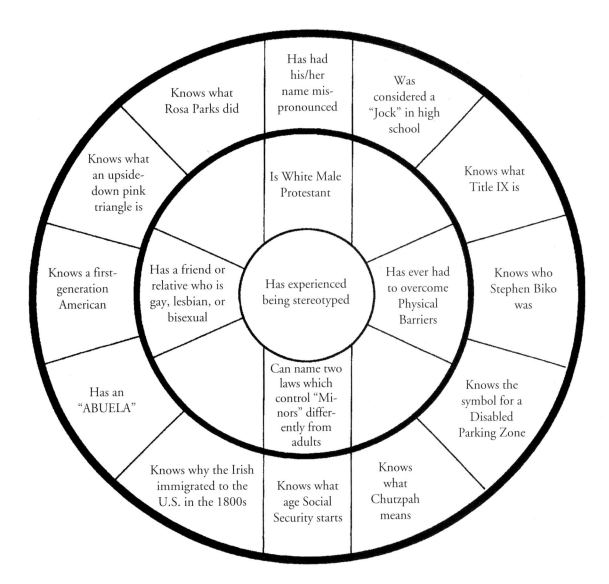

Directions: Locate an individual in the class who knows the answer to a question on the circle. Write that person's name in the block. Use each person only once.

Exercise 3.3 What Do You Know about Minority Groups?

1. A dulcimer is:
   a. An Appalachian folk instrument
   b. One who is low in spirits
   c. An Italian term of endearment
   d. A Native American weapon

2. The meaning of "Wounded Knee" is that:
   a. Native Americans in the 19th century viewed this as the last battle and a significant break in relationships with whites
   b. It was a rallying point for Native American militancy in the 1960s and 1970s
   c. None of the above
   d. Both a and b

3. A barrio is a:
   a. Political organization
   b. A small donkey
   c. Spanish speaking community
   d. None of the above

4. The letters "AME" are an abbreviation for:
   a. Anti-migration Effort
   b. American Muslim Enterprises
   c. African Methodist Episcopal
   d. Association of Moderate Encounters

5. Puerto Rico is an independent territory of the United States with self-governing powers.
   a. True
   b. False

6. A noted Chicano labor organizer and leader was:
   a. Pancho Villa
   b. Manuel Cortez
   c. Cesar Chavez
   d. Simon Bolivar

7. Name three prominent African-American writers:

8. According to most studies, what portion of the population in the United States is gay or lesbian?
   a. 1 in 50
   b. 1 in 10
   c. 1 in 100
   d. 1 in 5

9. The gay student organization on campus is called "Stonewall." What is the significance of this name?

10. Major league baseball did not allow any Black players until:
   a. 1925
   b. 1961
   c. 1947
   d. 1938

11. Match the following names with their achievements:

   _____ Arthur Ashe   a. wrote *Frankenstein*

   _____ Jim Thorpe   b. Gay author and activist

   _____ Jackie Robinson   c. Pilot who set speed records

   _____ Thurgood Marshall   d. First Black man to win US Open

   _____ Mary Shelley   e. First Black to win academy award

   _____ Frances Perkins   f. Native American Olympic athlete

   _____ Hattie McDaniel   g. First woman to hold Cabinet office

   _____ Randy Shilts   h. First Black Supreme Court justice

   _____ Henry Cisneros   i. First Hispanic mayor of major city

   _____ Jackie Cochran   j. First Black major league player

Name _____ Date _____

The questions below are intended to help you think and talk about your background and experiences, and learn about the experiences of other students in your class.

Instructions:
1. Form a **random** group of three students.
2. Each student should take a few minutes to complete the chart below.
3. When everyone in the group completes the chart, have each person read his/her responses to the members of the group (members should feel free to ask questions, share experiences).
4. Each student will share with the remainder of the class something interesting learned about another student's background.

Who are we?

My full name:	
The name I prefer to be called:	
The cultural meaning of my name:	
My ethnic identity:	
Place(s) my grandparents and parents were born:	
The language(s) I speak:	
My family's educational achievements:	
A person I admire:	
An attribute I like about myself or am proud of:	
A characteristic I like about my culture:	
A challenge I would like to conquer this semester:	
A challenge I would like to achieve in my lifetime:	

Adapted from materials created by The National Conference's "Actions Speak Louder: A Skills-Based Curriculum for Building Inclusion," 1995.

CHAPTER 4

Studying Effectively

"Leadership and learning are indispensable to each other."
—John F. Kennedy

Learning Styles • • • • • • • • • • • • • •

How do you learn? You've probably discovered by now that you have a certain way of learning and understanding what you hear and read. You probably also have a certain time of day when you prefer to study. It is a fact that there are "morning people" and "night people" when it comes to studying. This explains why some people are always up at the crack of dawn, take their classes as early as possible, and try to complete all of their homework assignments before dinner. On the other hand, there are those who stay up until dawn, schedule classes in the afternoon or at night, and prefer to study long after everyone else has gone to bed.

Where you choose to study can be as important as the time of day to successful studying. Where do you like to study? Are you a "library" person or an "in my room" person? Do you like absolute quiet or background noise? So, how do you learn? What is your learning style?

Let's begin our exploration of study skills with an assessment of your basic habits and preferences. Take a few minutes to complete items one through twelve

in Exercise 4.1. BE HONEST WITH YOURSELF! How do you **usually** behave in the situations described?

You now have some information that can be used in planning your approach to studying and learning. Let's develop a quick summary of your preferences so that you can refer back whenever you need a reminder. In the section provided in the exercise, write a brief summary statement which describes your preferred learning style.

Active Learning • • • • • • • • • • • • • • •

We all have different ways of learning the content presented in any class. Some of us learn best by listening, while others learn best by reading or by discussing. It is not coincidental that the three most popular teaching strategies in a university involve these three modes of learning.

Many students do not think about learning as an active process, one that requires some involvement on their part. Listening and reading are often considered passive activities, yet each requires active participation in order to provide maximum learning. Just as you have a preference for where and when you study, you also have a preference for how you study.

How do you learn best? What is your preferred learning preference or "style"? Take a few minutes to complete Exercise 4.2 about learning preferences. As you complete this exercise, consider how your learning preferences influence how you study and how you learn.

Reading •

When we ask students to tell us the title of the last book they read for fun, they seem to consider this a trick question. The words "read" and "fun" do not, from their perspective, fit logically together in the same sentence! The sad truth is that many students do not enjoy any form of reading including newspaper, magazines, and light fiction. We know, however, that "light" reading is a foundation for vocabulary development, understanding how a sentence and a paragraph are constructed, and expanding one's own imagination.

Many students, and even many who consider themselves effective readers, are overwhelmed by the amount of assigned reading and the complexity of ideas presented in their college texts. New vocabulary, new theories, and new concepts are presented in textbooks which provide the foundation for class discussion and understanding the professor's lectures. It is essential, therefore, to keep up with reading assignments; more important, it is necessary to approach reading as an active process that you engage in on a daily basis.

How many of the active strategies identified in Exercise 4.3 do you use when reading a text? Do you vary your approach to reading depending on the subject matter? At the end of the term, does your text look as if it has been used? Or is it still in pristine condition, containing little more than your name on the inside cover?

Active readers write in their books; active readers highlight, underline, and make notes in the margins; active readers write down questions to ask in class, either to clarify a point or seek additional information. In short, active readers are engaged in the process of reading.

When you read assigned materials before attending class, lectures will begin to make more sense. You will find that you understand more about the concepts and theories presented; terminology will seem familiar. Because the professor's lectures usually augment the text, your understanding of the topic expands if you are doing the reading assignments. A person who uses listening as a primary learning mode will more quickly pick up on critical points and increase her understanding of the materials. Those who enjoy the give and take of class discussion will have more to offer and will better understand the points made by others if the reading assignments are completed in advance.

There are many reading strategies and techniques designed to improve your reading skills if you find it difficult to keep up with assignments or do not fully understand the materials presented. Most campuses have a learning center or study skills center where a reading specialist can provide you with a diagnostic test and assist you in improving your reading speed and comprehension.

LEARNING CENTER

Location:_____

Telephone: _____

Hours: _____

Listening to Lectures ••••••••••••

Lectures are an efficient way for a professor to present new information not found in the text or to elaborate on materials that may have been covered superficially. While some professors may appear to repeat verbatim what is written in the text, most do not. Missing a lecture can mean missing important information which may appear later on a quiz or final exam. It has been said that 80 to 90 percent of the material on the average college exam is based on materials covered in class lectures and discussions. Attending class regularly is the most effective way to master subject materials. The notes you take will augment the readings and class discussions, and will serve to clarify ideas and concepts.

Listening to a lecture is not a passive activity. While sitting in a chair in a classroom is fairly passive, the process of sitting and **listening** is not. The first and most important step in developing good listening skills is to attend every class session on time! Or, as one student was fond of saying, "You snooze, you lose!"

The most visible activity during a lecture is notetaking. Less obvious to the casual observer is the thinking process which determines which words or phrases finally appear in a student's notes. Try the following experiment with one of your friends in a class you take in common. See how the two of you "hear" the same lecture!

Critical listening requires careful attention to what is said. It goes beyond hearing words and requires an understanding of the meanings behind what is said. If terminology is unfamiliar or concepts are unclear, your level of learning will be reduced. In fact, it is not uncommon to hear a student say after a lecture, "I didn't understand anything she said." An important part of effective listening is asking for clarification when you don't understand something.

Many students are reluctant to ask questions in class because they don't want to appear unknowledgeable, "uncool," or, even worse, foolish. In fact, every time you have a question, you may safely assume that at least 30 percent of the class has a similar question in mind. How often has someone asked a question that you, too, were considering? This leads to the importance of class discussion in the learning process.

Classroom Discussion • • • • • • • • • •

Most college professors welcome and encourage class participation. In many classes, discussion plays a vital part in the learning process. It is also the mechanism used by professors for identifying and exploring points which are unclear to students. Discussion provides an opportunity to examine different perspectives or points of view.

As we mentioned earlier, students are responsible for asking questions when information is unclear. If you have read your assignment, listened attentively, and still do not understand, ask questions of the professor. Most professors enjoy answering questions and view them as a sign of student involvement.

If you find it difficult to ask questions in class, make it a point to talk with the professor after class or during his office hours. Seeking clarification is the student's responsibility. A professor cannot tell by looking at you whether or not you understand the subject under discussion; if you wait to see how you do on the exam, it may be too late!

This active approach applies to other types of class participation. Many professors structure their classes in such a way that participation is required. This allows the professor to see students in action and promotes a lively learning environment. While there are some students in every class who will not participate, and there are students who participate without being adequately prepared, most seem to enjoy and benefit from an active involvement in the learning process.

In a class where participation in discussions is a part of the grading system, it is important to find ways to contribute to each and every class session. While you do not have to talk all of the time, contribute your thoughts and ideas as appropriate.

Integrated Learning • • • • • • • • • • • •

The most successful students are those who learn to integrate the three primary learning modes. They read, listen, and participate, using each mode as needed for the subject and structure of the course. These students develop habits that fit their individual learning style and increase their chance for success in the classroom. While each successful student has a dominate or "preferred" approach to learning, each

Note Taking Experiment

During one of your class sessions, each of you take notes as you usually do. After class, have a cup of coffee together and compare your notes to see what information each of you thought was important. Compare the format of your notes for clarity and future use as a study tool in preparing for exams.

What did you learn from this experiment? Is one of you a better note taker? Did you "hear" the same information? Could you benefit from exchanging notes on a regular basis? More on note taking later!

has learned to use the other modes in support. Let's consider some specific strategies and techniques to improve learning.

Developing Study Skills •••••••••

Do you have one or two friends who never seem to study but always manage to get good grades? They are probably brilliant or lucky, or maybe they have developed effective study habits. Possibly all three conditions apply! In fact, many successful students have developed such good study habits that they never appear to study at all. They have time for a social life, participation in activities, and, perhaps, even a job. How do they do it?

Assuming you have identified a place or two where you feel comfortable studying and you have some ideas about which modes of learning you prefer, the next challenge is actually sitting down and doing it. This is the point at which students begin to have difficulties. Let's examine a few of the reasons why effective studying can be so difficult.

Distractions •••••••••••••••••••

No matter how carefully you've selected that ideal study location and how motivated you are, there will be some distractions every time you prepare to study.

These may be self-created: day dreaming, thinking about other things you need or want to do, feeling overwhelmed by the amount of studying you have to get done. Or the distractions may be external: background noises, other people entering the area, not having on hand the information or materials you need.

Distractions often become an excuse for not making good use of study time, so you have to become aware of what distracts you and develop ways to address these distractions as they occur. Good study habits begin with an ability to focus on the task at hand, no matter what.

Attitude ••••••••••••••••••••••••

Do you view studying a "chore" to be done? A punishment? If you see it this way, studying will not seem enjoyable in any way. If all study time is viewed as unpleasant, you will resent being put in this situation and will, at some level, resist.

Students who resist or resent time spent preparing for classes, reviewing notes, and reading are probably negative about school in general. They find studying as one more "chore." If you are a student who has this attitude about studying, then perhaps attending college may not be the right thing for you right now! However, if you want to be in college and have goals that include a college degree, then it is time to consider your attitudes about studying.

Five Ways to Improve Your Academic Performance

1. Read a good novel for an hour each day instead of watching TV. It will improve both your reading and writing skills.
2. Write all of your papers on a computer with spell check. **Use spell check!**
3. Let a paper sit for at least three days before preparing a final copy. Careless errors will become more visible.
4. Learn three new words a week and use them. Just using a dictionary is helpful.
5. Don't let a job or your social life become more important than school. If school is not your number-one priority right now, why are you here?

Motivation • • • • • • • • • • • • • • • •

Effective students are usually highly motivated people. They have set clear goals for themselves and are excited and challenged by the process of learning. College is viewed as an opportunity to explore exciting new interests and ideas.

Motivation is something that is intrinsic. No one else can motivate you, although others in your life may support and encourage your efforts. Sometimes another person, perhaps a professor or another student, will challenge or inspire you, but that's different from the basic motivation to learn, which has to come from within.

Competing Demands • • • • • • • • • • •

Most students do have a life outside of attending classes and studying, but what is that "life"? If too many things are competing for your time and attention, studying and attending class may begin to drop off your list of priorities. The "big three" competitors for students' time are jobs for pay, friends, and family. If the time required for any (or all) of these interferes with your study time and going to classes, it is likely you will never become as successful a student as you might like to be.

How do you say, "No" to family and friends? How do you give up all those things that your job allows you to buy or pay for? The answer is simple: it takes practice, a willingness to make changes in your life, and a commitment to planning for the future rather than living only in the here-and-now.

A Few Study Tips • • • • • • • • • • • • • •

Now that we've looked at some of the factors in your life that might interfere with serious, productive study, let's examine some of the basic skill areas required to be a successful student. Mastery of basic study skills is the second major problem area for students after the intrinsic issues are addressed. Entire books have been written on each of the following topics. This is a brief starting point for you to begin developing your skills as needed.

Five characteristics consistently demonstrated by successful managers working for the Xerox Corporation were, in no particular order:

Creativity
Inquisitiveness
Idealism
Ability to change
A sense of values and ethics

The Three "R's" • • • • • • • • • • • • • • •

It may seem simplistic, but the foundation of all successful academic work is mastery of those skills you were first taught in your earliest education: reading, writing, and mathematics. If you are not a good reader, cannot write effectively, and shy away from anything mathematical, you are in for a challenging experience in college!

Very few college classes, for example, are taught without a designated textbook or two. Often, several additional books will be assigned as reserved reading in the library. To cover this amount of written material, you must read quickly and with reasonable levels of comprehension. Students who are not strong readers might benefit from taking a course designed to improve reading speed and comprehension. Such courses may be taken at a community college or you might want to schedule time with a reading specialist in the university's learning center.

Writing is another major requirement in most college courses. Many universities now insist that all students demonstrate a mastery of basic writing skills as a requirement for graduation. This may mean taking a specific sequence of writing courses or it may mean passing a test of your English writing skills.

You will write papers in almost every course you take. Some professors will reduce your grade if a paper is poorly written from a technical perspective. If you don't use proper sentence structure, punctuation, and spelling, your grade may be dropped significantly. While you will focus much of your attention on a paper's content, it cannot be the sole consideration in preparing college-level written assignments. You need to learn to write clearly, concisely, and correctly.

If you don't own a basic style manual, buy one. There are several available and in general use including the **Chicago Manual of Style**, the **Modern Language Association Manual of Style**, and the **American Psychological Association Style Manual**. A style manual will provide you with the correct technical information required to write a strong paper.

Mathematics is another subject required for graduation from most universities. While the number of required courses may vary, it is not uncommon for students to fulfill both basic math and computer literacy requirements. Many academic majors require more. Students whose math background is weak need to take lower-level preparatory courses before tackling college-level courses if they hope to be successful. Math is one of those areas where there is no substitute for mastery of the basic skills!

Using Placement Test Scores • • • • •

At Orientation, you took placement tests that provided some information about your preparation for college-level math and/or writing courses. You may have taken one or more Advanced Placement (AP) International Baccalaureate (IB) or College Level Examination Program (CLEP) tests before coming to the university. These tests may have provided you with credits for college-level course work in one or more areas and allow you to immediately move on to higher level courses.

If you took a placement test, however, you may dislike the results and want to take more advanced courses than the recommended placement level. We're not sure whether this reluctance to accept placement results is "ego" or just difficulty in admitting a weakness in earlier academic preparation. The reasons are irrelevant. What is important to understand is that students who ignore placement test results and individually choose to enroll in higher-level courses often fail those courses.

Placement tests can help identify areas where you may need additional work to become as effective in the classroom as you might like to be. Don't ignore the results of these tests because of your vanity!

Listening Skills • • • • • • • • • • • • • •

When you are not reading or writing, the odds are you will be in a classroom listening. You will listen to lectures, class discussions, and speeches by guest lecturers. Each form of oral communication will reinforce or add to what you've read and researched. Listening effectively is a critical and difficult skill to develop. It is related to a number of factors including your ability to focus and concentrate.

Where do you sit in class? What is your in-class "attitude?" Are you attentive? Do you follow what is going on? Are you day-dreaming? Dozing? Worrying about what you'll be doing after dinner? These things all influence your ability to focus and learn from what you are hearing.

Note Taking • • • • • • • • • • • • • • • • •

There are many different systems of note taking. Any basic study skills book can provide you a "system" for taking notes during class and when you are reading the text. There are, however, some common elements in all systems.

A first step is to **develop and use** a system of note taking that you understand and can interpret. There is nothing worse than looking at notes a week or two later and discovering that you have no idea what they mean! Individual note taking systems often include:

1. Developing a set of abbreviations that you can use as a form of "shorthand." This saves time when taking notes, but is only effective if you can remember what your symbols mean.

2. Not writing down everything. Look for key words, definitions, terms, and new concepts. Most professors work from an outline while lecturing, even if they sometimes digress. Try to follow and take notes in an outline format.

3. Leaving space to add new information or continue points on a topic that may appear at a later time in the lecture.

4. Reviewing your notes within 24 hours after the class. It is easier to make additions and clarifications while the information is still fresh in your mind. You can also identify questions to ask at the next class session.

Figure 4.1 Common Abbreviations

&	=	and
%	=	percent
>	=	greater than
<	=	less than
♀	=	woman, female
♂	=	man, male
w/	=	with
w/o	=	without
=	=	equals

One popular system of note taking which many students use is outlined in Figure 4.2. There are notebooks and note paper which are formatted to use this type of note taking approach.

Test Taking • • • • • • • • • • • • • • • • • •

Tests take on a new meaning in college. In some ways, universities still follow the old academic tradition in which tests were the primary mechanism for determining who received a degree and who did not. Students attended lectures until they (and their "tutor") decided they were ready to take examinations. Those who passed were awarded a degree; those who failed left the university. Some students attended lectures for years without ever taking their examinations or earning a degree!

Instructors and Testing • • • • • • • • •

Taking tests is one of the most challenging parts of any course. No matter how well you read or how precise your notes might be, tests and quizzes will make up a large part of your grade in most classes. And, unfortunately, there will be fewer tests upon which your grade is based than you were accustomed to in high school. Some professors may give only two exams, a mid-term and final. Other professors may give several quizzes in addition to a mid-term and final. Then there is that occasional class when the only test is a final!

Professors may also weigh tests or quizzes differently. A final may count for as much as one-half of the course grade or it may be weighed the same as any other test or quiz given during the course. Some professors count every test grade, while others allow students to "throw out" their lowest grade. Some professors allow make-up tests if you miss an exam; others do not.

As a student, you have to learn each professor's testing system, expectations, and requirements. Unlike high school, there are few acceptable excuses for missing a test or quiz. You must negotiate with each instructor if something happens and you miss a test; however, don't expect much sympathy if you were not in contact *before* the test was given.

Types of Tests • • • • • • • • • • • • • • • •

Three common types of tests are essay, short-answer, and multiple-choice/true-false. Which type of test is given depends on the individual professor's preferences and, to some extent, the course material. Each test type requires a different strategy and study method. Knowing what type of test the instructor gives will allow you to better prepare yourself.

Essay tests are often given in courses where students are expected to analyze and compare or contrast information. When preparing for an essay test, keep the following points in mind:

1. Read each question carefully and understand what is required in your response. More points are deducted for not understanding directions than for any other reason. Look for key words

Figure 4.2 Important Developmental Theories

Review chapters on
Kohlberg and Perry

Piaget - infancy
early childhood
(look up)

Check spellings r
Names - Chapt. 6 ?

IMPORTANT DEVELOPMENTAL THEORIES

1. Kohlberg : MORAL DEVELOPMENT
2. PERRY : INT'L. DEV.
   - STAGES USED - 7
   - RESEARCH ON college students
3. CHICKERING : STUDENT DEV.
   - ALSO STAGES
   - INTELLECTUAL, social Dev,

Role of Development

1. LIFE span Dev.
   - Early childhood
   - ADOLESCENT Dev.
   X - ADULT DEV.

2. MANY NEW THEORIES OF
   ADULT DEV.
   - LEVINGER
   - SHEEHY (?)
   - LEVITT (?)

3. WHAT WE can learn from theory

NEXT CLASS : Chapter 7
     pp 281- 297

- Bring first short paper
(DUE WEDNESDAY)

and phrases like "compare," "contrast," and "describe," which suggest how your answer should be framed.

2. Take time to make some notes or a brief outline of ideas before you begin writing. Think about key points or concepts you want to include in your answer. Don't be in too big a hurry to begin writing.

3. Keep track of time if you have more than one essay question to answer. If points are evenly distributed for the questions, distribute your time evenly.

4. Use your best writing skills. Write in complete sentences using correct punctuation and spelling. Many instructors will deduct points for poor writing, regardless of how well you may cover the topic.

5. Leave enough time to review your answers. It is likely that you will recall additional information when you do this.

Short-answer tests are used most frequently in courses where clusters of information are important. Questions usually call for recollection of facts, dates, names, or lists of items. Short answer tests may also involve filling in blanks and writing one or two sentence responses.

In responding to questions on this type of test, consider the following points:

1. Read the sentence stem or question carefully. Be sure you understand what type of information is sought. Ask yourself what you recall from readings and lectures about the topic.

2. Be brief and focused in your responses. That's why this is called a "short-answer" test!

3. Jot down ideas in the margin or on the back of the test before you start responding. Organize your ideas by looking at all of the questions and making some notes before you start writing.

4. Start with the items you know best and leave the more difficult questions until last. Successfully completing one or two questions will relax you and probably help you recall additional information.

Multiple-choice tests are often used in large lecture sections and for common departmental exams. These tests are usually machine scored and make use of standard computer answer sheets. When taking a multiple choice or true-false test, the following suggestions may be helpful:

1. Read the directions carefully. If a computer answer sheet is used, examine the format and know which way the numbers go. Some use horizontal and some use vertical numbering. A quick way to fail a test is to bubble in the right answer next to an incorrect number!

2. Don't panic if you don't know the answer to the first item or two. Keep reading and begin with those answers you do know.

3. Unless there is a penalty for guessing, answer every item on the test. With true-false questions, you have a 50-50 chance of guessing correctly; with multiple choice responses, you can often rule out some of the response options and narrow your choices.

4. As you work through the test, look for information that may assist you in answering other questions.

5. As a rule of thumb, don't change answers unless you are certain the new answer is correct. Your first choice is usually the better choice if you are not 100 percent certain.

Using Study Groups •••••••••••

In many courses, forming a study group is an effective way to master subject material. There are some distinct advantages to study groups as well as some potential drawbacks.

On the positive side, study groups offer support, a chance to hear others' ideas, and an opportunity to test your own knowledge through the give-and-take of group discussion. On the down side, study groups can become an excuse for not keeping up with assignments, a social rather than a work group, or a mechanism for letting others do the work. Study groups are definitely not for everyone.

Groups are best used in courses where there is much reading. Discussing a reading assignment can be helpful in developing a deeper understanding of the material. Groups are also helpful in courses where memorization and repetition may be required. Group members can "coach" one another, develop practice questions, and quiz one another.

Follow these basic guidelines for a successful group experience:

1. Know who is joining the group. Every member should be willing to make a commitment of both time and effort. If not, you may be the one doing all the work!
2. Establish a regular meeting time and place. Try to avoid areas where people are socializing (the cafeteria, the student center lounge).
3. Agree on how the group will function. Will members each take special responsibility for some aspect of the assignment? Will everyone come prepared to discuss the entire assignment? Will someone lead the discussion?
4. How will the group deal with non-participation? With people who don't do their part of the work?
5. Will you share and discuss writing assignments in the group? (Remember, written work you submit as part of a class assignment must be your own, but the group can give feedback on what you've written.)

More Than Just Books

Books, magazines, a place to study or meet friends—that's what most students think of when they think about libraries. But university libraries are much more: research collections of all kinds and in various formats; services to help you do your assignments and write your papers; and people who are detectives at finding information and committed to teaching you how to become information literate. The library is the heart of academic life and your gateway to the world of information. In a later chapter we will discuss ways to develop your "information literacy."

Summary

Being a good student requires time and effort on your part. It begins with knowing yourself and how you best learn information. Good students also develop basic skills and strategies that allow them to manage their workload successfully. Assess your study habits now and begin to make the kinds of changes that will enhance your performance in the classroom.

Name _____ Date_____

Write the letter of the *best* answer in the space.

_____   1. I study best when I'm working
              a. alone.
              b. with a friend.
              c. in a group.

_____   2. My energy level is highest
              a. early in the morning.
              b. in mid-afternoon.
              c. late at night.

_____   3. I concentrate best
              a. in total silence.
              b. with the radio or television on.
              c. with normal noise and confusion around me.

_____   4. I learn best if I
              a. highlight or underline important material in the text.
              b. say or make important points aloud.
              c. write important information in my own words.

_____   5. I study best when I'm
              a. reclining in bed.
              b. sitting at a table or desk.
              c. relaxing in a comfortable chair.

_____   6. I learn best when I study
              a. in long blocks of time.
              b. in several short blocks of time with short breaks.
              c. in no set pattern.

_____   7. I study best when the room is
              a. warm and cozy.
              b. a little cool.
              c. about normal temperature.

_____   8. I usually work best
              a. with dim lighting.
              b. with bright lights all around me.
              c. with normal lighting.

_____   9. After studying a long time, I find I relax best by
              a. reading something light.
              b. exercising.
              c. visiting with friends.

_____ 10. I function best if I
  a. get eight or more hours of sleep a night.
  b. get only a few hours of sleep and nap occasionally during the day.
  c. vary the amount of sleep I get in relation to my activities.

_____ 11. I work best
  a. under pressure.
  b. when relaxed.

_____ 12. I can handle well
  a. only one thing at a time.
  b. many projects simultaneously.

Summary of my learning style: _____

_____

_____

_____

_____

_____

_____

_____

_____

_____

_____

_____

················· **Exercise 4.2 Self-Awareness Inventory** ················

Choose the answer that is usually true for you, even though more than one answer might be appropriate sometimes. Write the letter in the space.

_____ 1. When taking notes from a lecture, I usually
   a. try to write down everything.
   b. randomly select some of the ideas.
   c. identify and write down the important points.

_____ 2. When studying for an exam from my class notes, I usually find the notes
   a. incomprehensible.
   b. incomplete.
   c. adequate.

_____ 3. When I study, I usually
   a. need to get up and get supplies (dictionary, paper, pencil, etc.) frequently.
   b. have everything I need but get up because I'm restless.
   c. get down to work without frequent breaks because I have everything I need.

_____ 4. If I don't understand something, I usually
   a. avoid it, hoping I'll get by.
   b. ask someone about it.
   c. try to figure it out.

_____ 5. When I read a chapter in my textbook, I usually
   a. read it straight through, giving my equal attention to each word.
   b. skip through it and read the parts that interest me.
   c. try to pick out the major points.

_____ 6. When I come to illustrations or other graphic aids in the textbook, I usually
   a. skip over them.
   b. glance at them casually.
   c. try to relate them to the narrative portion of the text.

_____ 7. When I try to remember material for an exam, I usually
   a. rely on memory tricks.
   b. make silly associations.
   c. relate new material to what I already know.

_____ 8. I prepare for exams by
   a. cramming the night before the exam.
   b. completing each assignment when it is due.
   c. completing assignments when due and reviewing periodically.

_____ 9. On an exam, I usually
   a. answer each question as I come to it.
   b. concentrate on the most difficult questions.
   c. work quietly through the exam, answering questions I'm sure of first.

10. When taking a test, the questions are usually
    a. a complete surprise.
    b. some that I expected and others that I did not anticipate.
    c. about what I expected them to be.

11. If I want to find a specific topic in my book, I am likely to
    a. flip through the pages hunting for it randomly.
    b. look in the table of contents.
    c. look in the index.

12. When I go to the library, I
    a. seldom know how to find what I need.
    b. usually ask for help in locating materials.
    c. usually find what I want.

13. When I need to study but I'm tempted to do something else, I usually
    a. give in to temptation.
    b. compromise—do a little of both.
    c. study.

14. I work best when
    a. someone tells me exactly what to do and checks up on me.
    b. I follow the same plan for every assignment.
    c. I work at my own pace and in my own way.

15. When the teacher calls on me unexpectedly during class, I usually
    a. guess at the answer.
    b. go blank.
    c. give the right answer.

16. When studying for an exam, I usually
    a. run out of time.
    b. have time left over.
    c. have about the right amount of time.

17. If I want to get good grades, I have to
    a. study nearly all the time.
    b. give up my social life.
    c. carefully balance my time between studying and extra-curricular activities.

18. If I have a term paper to write, I
    a. wait until the last minute.
    b. am not sure how to proceed.
    c. organize the assignment and meet self-imposed deadlines.

19. When I think about my course work, I generally feel
    a. that it is a waste of time.
    b. discouraged and depressed.
    c. that I'm learning something worthwhile.

_____ 20. When the teacher assigns homework, I usually
  a. try to get out of doing it.
  b. resent the assignment but do it anyway.
  c. do it because it will probably help me learn what I need to know.

_____ 21. When it's time to go to class, I usually
  a. dread going.
  b. go because attendance is required.
  c. go to learn something.

_____ 22. When I don't understand an assignment, I'm likely to
  a. not do it.
  b. do it any way I can.
  c. ask for clarification.

Answers to Exercise 4.2

The "a" response indicates poor approaches to learning, while the "c" responses indicate good approaches. The "b" responses are neither good nor bad indicators. In evaluating your learning habits, consider that 10 or more "a" responses suggest you need to review and revise your approach to studying. Ten or more "c" responses suggest you already employ some effective habits.

The Inventory items are divided into several categories. In analyzing your answers by category, you may identify some areas where change will be helpful. The items and categories are:

1–4	Study skills
5–6	Textbook reading
7–10	Exams
11–12	Reference skills
13–14	Self-discipline
15–16	Stress
17–19	Time management
20–23	Attitude

·············· # Exercise 4.3 Active Reading Strategies ··············

Reading a textbook is not like reading a novel; reading a novel is not like reading the newspaper. Much of the reading you'll do in the next few years will be linked to textbooks and assignments for college courses, so let's assess your level of skill for this type of reading.

As you read each of the following statements, mark your response using this key:

> 1 = I seldom or never do this.
> 2 = I occasionally do this, depending on the class.
> 3 = I almost always or always do this.

_____   1. I write notes in the margin of the text.

_____   2. I underline or highlight important phrases and passages.

_____   3. Before I begin reading, I glance through the chapter and note section headings.

_____   4. I read the summary of the chapter before reading the chapter.

_____   5. I take notes in my notebook for future study as I read.

_____   6. I keep up with reading assignments on a daily basis.

_____   7. I re-read chapter summaries before tests.

_____   8. I plan reading time for each class in my weekly schedule.

_____   9. I review reading assignments and lecture notes after class to be certain I understand everything.

_____   10. If a chapter has study questions, I use them as a guide.

TOTAL POINTS: _____

Scoring Key: 25–30 points   You're a skilled reader!
                20–24 points   You're good but keep improving.
                15–19 points   Some changes are needed.
                10–14 points   Major improvements are needed.
                 0–9 points   Seek assistance!

CHAPTER 5

Managing Information

*"Good communication is as stimulating as black
coffee and just as hard to sleep after."*
—Anne Morrow Lindberg

Libraries and the World of Information ••••••••••••••

Welcome to the world of libraries, the heart of the university and your gateway to the world of information. Academic libraries are more than books, magazines and a place to study or meet friends. Libraries contain collections of all kinds and in various formats; services to help you do your assignments and write your papers; computers to connect you to databases of information as well as to the World Wide Web; and people who are detectives at finding information and committed to teaching you how to become information literate.

The computers in libraries will connect you to the local library's online catalog, other libraries' online catalogs, and commercial online services and will provide access to the Internet and the World Wide Web. Each library has its own set of computer services and training sessions and tutorials to help you use all of the computer resources available.

This chapter will introduce you to some library basics that you need to know **now** to make your life a lot less hectic while improving the overall quality of your work. Your library probably offers all types of classes, workshops and online tutorials to further help you become information literate. Becoming information literate will require that you continue to learn about other library resources and services as you pursue your college career.

Information Literacy ••••••••••

In order to function successfully in today's society, you must be not only **literate** (able to read), but also **information literate** (able to find, evaluate and use information effectively). Information is packaged in all kinds of formats, including electronic formats, so **computer literacy** (basic technical computer skills) is a necessary component to becoming information literate.

Your first step is an orientation to the staff, services and collection in **your** library. Next, there are steps to follow when looking for information sources. Finally, the basics of evaluating sources to be sure you have what you need for your project or paper are discussed.

First Things First ••••••••••••••

Universities often have more than one library that may or may not function as one library system. For example, if your university has campuses located in different geographic locations, there may be libraries on each campus. Many larger or older universities have subject libraries for each college (e.g., science, music, or law) or there may be a separate undergraduate library. You need to find out if the libraries are divided and where resources are located.

All libraries have different kinds of service desks to assist you. Some of these service desks include: Circulation; Reserve; Information; Periodicals; Reference; Government Documents; and Audio/Visual. At each service desk you can receive help using specific materials or services. The Information Desk is usually a good place to discover where services are provided in your library.

Librarians and their staff are available in most library locations to help you with your research. It is important to know that there are different levels of staff employed by libraries. Librarians are generally available at a Reference Desk and in Government Documents. Librarians are experts at finding out exactly what it is you need. They will also teach you how to find it. In many libraries, students may even make an appointment for extended assistance with a librarian.

Most libraries now have an online orientation program. This program will explain how to use your academic library and its services. Knowing library hours and locations, how to access the online catalog from your dorm or home, and where to go to get assistance are first steps to becoming **information literate.**

Online Library Catalogs •••••••••

Library catalogs used to be in card files with individual cards for each item in the library's book collection. Now a catalog includes resources available to all users on the World Wide Web. From your computer you can now access your library's collection of books, many magazine articles, other sources, and the resources of other libraries, as well. Online library catalogs allow searches by author, title, and subject; most have key word searching; and some allow full text

This chapter was written by Dr. Elizabeth J. McNeer, a consultant and former library director. It is used by permission of the author.

searching of specialized materials. The online records will provide a location and whether the materials are currently available, on reserve, or checked out at the time of the search. The library's home page will also show you the extent of the resources available through the online catalog. The librarians will have handouts and tutorials to explain the use of the library's online catalog.

Finding Information • • • • • • • • • • •

The next step, finding information, requires that you define your topic and the focus of your research project or paper. In most cases, you will have many specific questions that make up your larger question. There is often so much information available on any one topic, that you need to determine how much information you really need to find, and how technical the information needs to be. Identifying all the questions that you need to answer in order to complete your project is an important step in becoming **information literate**.

In order to begin a research project, you must be able to clearly state the information you need and the type of sources you think you will need to use. Even when your research project is not due until the end of the term, it is to your advantage to begin searching for sources as soon as the project is assigned. You will be competing with other students for information resources and for the time of the librarians to help you. Also, if the library does not own the materials that are needed, you will have to ask the library to order the information from other libraries. This will also take time. **Begin searching early!**

Defining your project means writing a clear **topic sentence**. This is an excellent way to define what information you might need, how much information you might need, and how technical the information needs to be. If you are unsure of how to write a topic sentence, try using the search strategy worksheet to define your topic. As you find sources of information for your paper or project, you will continue to refine your topic sentence and the focus of your project.

Sources of Information • • • • • • • • • •

There are many sources of information that you can find in the library. In addition to books and magazines, there are scholarly journals in which professors and scholars publish the results of their research, newspapers, indexes to magazines, newspapers and journal articles; government documents from the state, federal, and international agencies; and fact books and specialized reference sources for each discipline. There are sources which provide only factual data and others which provide opinions. There are sources chosen for undergraduate students to use in their research and others which only graduate students and faculty will find useful. All the resources in libraries are chosen after a review process designed to meet the academic and scholarly needs of students and faculty. The librarians at the Reference Desk can help you choose the most appropriate sources, **if you can define your research project.**

Using the World Wide Web • • • • • •

The "Information Age" has become a period of intense effort to transform libraries from physical places where books and other materials are stored to connections to information and services that you can access by computer from home or office. We are in a period of transition as we move from a print to an electronic information environment. The current generation of students and scholars must cope with this transition while learning to use ALL formats of information.

The World Wide Web is an independent way to publish and present information that is open to anyone who has access to the Internet. No one dictates what information is loaded on the Web or how it is presented. While the lack of authoritative review ensures that opinions, ideas and creative presentations are available on the Web, not everything found on the Web is useful for academic research.

While you are a student, you will use the Web for many different types of information retrieval. For example, your university's Home Page will give you access to information about the college, the courses and programs available, and the rules and regulations you need to follow. Access to registration, class schedules and grades are among the important uses of your university's Web information. Schedules for plays, concerts, sports events, and other campus activities can also be found on the Web page as well.

Increasingly colleges are offering some of their courses on the Web or in Web-assisted courses such as WEBCT, Blackboard, TopClass, or Intralearn. When a student is enrolled in one of these Web-assisted courses, the syllabus, assignment and tests are available online. Most Web-assisted courses include email and chat room components. Many students enjoy the Web-assisted parts of their courses as much as they enjoy the classroom sessions.

Figure 5.1

Searching the Library and the Web—A Strategy

1. **Topic**
   Can you express your topic in a sentence or a question? Are there broader or narrower aspects to your topic? What related terms might provide more information in your search?

2. **Background Information**
   What do you already know about your topic? Can you use your textbook or other resources for background information? What have you read about your topic in other classes?

3. **Begin Searching for Information**
   Use the library's online catalog to begin your search. Locate journal articles and other online sources. Be sure to evaluate Internet sources carefully.

4. **Review Your Results**
   Have you found too much information? Narrow your topic or limit the sources you will use.

   Have you found too little information? Look at a broader aspect of the topic. Return to Steps 1–3.

5. **Evaluate the Sources**
   Select the best sources for the purpose of your project or paper.

Using the Internet ••••••••••••

The World Wide Web provides access to a vast array of information to all users. Information on the Web is organized on web pages. The first page in a set of web pages is called the home page. To search the Internet for information contained on web pages, you must utilize a search engine. Search engines differ in the amount and type of web pages they scan to locate topics you are researching. Librarians can suggest appropriate searching strategies. Experience with Internet searching will help you know which search engine can help you with your research.

Among the most useful sources on the World Wide Web are the home pages for governmental agencies (.gov), educational institutions (.edu), and private organizations (.org). Often their research results appear on the Internet before they are available in print. Governmental agencies provide statistics on most topics and educational institutions and private organizations report on the latest research in their fields of expertise.

A useful item you will need to begin a search on the World Wide Web is that **topic sentence** discussed above. The **key words** in that topic sentence can be used as the basis for a search. If they do not produce the type of information you need, synonyms or other terms may be needed. The Librarians at the Reference Desk can also help you with Internet searching.

Evaluating Sources ••••••••••••

Part of your college education is learning how to evaluate sources of information and make decisions about their usefulness to your papers and projects. University libraries contain the best books available for college students to use for their projects. University libraries also include many materials for graduate students and faculty that may not be appropriate for most undergraduates.

In any library, you should look for and check the date of any publication you select. If you need current data, many books may not be as useful as magazine

and newspaper articles. If you need an historical perspective, older books may provide better sources of data than more recent materials.

The authority of the author of the material you choose is also important. University professors publish many scholarly books, journal articles, and textbooks which are usually good sources of factual material. The bibliographies in their books and journal articles can lead you to other sources of scholarly materials.

Governmental agencies publish the results of surveys and studies that are excellent sources of current factual information. For example, the United States Census Bureau publishes the complete results of each decennial census with extensive information about our country and its people.

It is important to remember that authors of every source you locate in the library or on the web have presented their material to meet their own purpose. You need to be able to determine what that purpose is and whether or not you can use that material for your project.

For example, politicians and advocates of special interests publish books, articles, their own newspapers, and have web sites to provide their own view of issues and candidates. Their materials are a great source for a persuasive paper or a debate. But, your professors would not want you to base an entire factual paper on that type of source material, even if you agree with the author's point of view.

A factual presentation requires the presentation of all points of view on an issue, so more research is usually needed. Even for a persuasive paper or debate, you might need to view the material on the other side of the issue in order to present your view as the "best" one. Knowing the source and the author's point of view in the material you locate will help you to evaluate it effectively.

How good are you at evaluating sources? Exercise 5.2 provides an outline to assist you when you evaluate your sources.

Citations •••••••••••••••••••••

Footnotes, endnotes, and bibliographies are all types of citations to the sources you used to prepare your paper or project. When you use ideas, facts, and quotations from another source, you must give credit to that author. The complete information that you provide will allow your professor to locate, retrieve and read that same source you used.

There are a number of standard formats for citations and bibliographies. All formats require that you list the author, the date of the source material, the title of the source (book, journal, or Web site), and the publication data that will allow your professor to locate the materials you used. It is important that you make note of this information while you are doing your research, so that it is available when you are preparing your final draft of your paper or project. It is very difficult and time consuming to locate your reference sources again when you are typing your paper or project.

Your professors will have particular styles they prefer. There are style manuals available in the library with examples to show you how to list the research sources that you used to prepare your paper or project. Older style manuals may not contain examples of citations for Web resources. Check with your professor or the reference librarian for the proper form for your Web citations.

Figure 5.2

Checklist for Evaluating Sources

	Books	**Articles**	**WEB Pages**
Accuracy Facts correct?	What sources are cited?	What sources are cited?	Is the source of facts given?
Authority	What is the author's background?	What organization funded this research?	Is the author listed? What is the author's background?
Objectivity What is the bias of the source?	Who is the publisher?	Is the journal refereed?	What is the bias of the site? Is this a commercial site selling a product?
Currency Do you need up-to-date resources?	Date of publication? Is this the most recent edition?	Date of the study?	When last updated?
Coverage Are all aspects of topic included? Will you need more sources?	Is there a bibliography?	Can you use references to find more information?	Is this site complete? Are there links to other sites?

Summary ••••••••••••••••••••

Your college success is, to a large extent, dependent upon your skills at identifying, locating, and evaluating information in order to use it effectively. This is called **information literacy.** This chapter provided you an orientation to the library. First, you learned about the staff, services and collection in the library. Then you learned how to describe your topic sentence and locate materials in the library and on the World Wide Web to provide resources for your project. Finally, you learned the basics of evaluating the sources you found. You are now ready to apply these skills to all your research. Be sure to explore the opportunities provided at the library in order to expand your **information literacy** skills.

···················· **Exercise 5.1 Library Hunt** ····················

1. How many libraries are there on your campus?

2. What is the name of the library on your campus?

3. What are the library's regular hours?

4. Where did you find handouts about using this library?

5. Are there classes or workshops provided in the library? When is the next one offered?

6. Where is the information or reference desk in your library?

7. What is the name of the library's on line catalog?

8. Can you find books in other libraries using your library's online catalog?

9. What do you need as an undergraduate student to check out books? How long can you keep them?

10. How can you connect to the library from your home computer?

Exercise 5.2

When beginning a writing project that involves research, we often start with a topic and look for books or other materials that might tell us something about that topic. We want these source materials to have "authority" or present expert information.

Here is the title page and the acknowledgments page for a book. Look at these closely.

The Future of the Everglades

By

Lotta Waters, Ph.D.

University Press
2000

I would like to thank Professor Doctor and the members of my Committee at State University School of Environmental Studies for their assistance and critique of my doctoral thesis, which is the basis for this text. I would also like to thank the staff of the National Parks Service, the Fish and Wildlife Commission, the Audubon Society, and the Miccosukee Indian Tribe, whose assistance and advice was so helpful to me in gathering the facts and opinions presented in this book.

Imagine you have been assigned a research project on the Everglades. Based only on these two pages introducing this book, **The Future of the Everglades,** what kinds of evidence can you find about the authority of the author and the viewpoints she might present?

1. _____

2. _____

3. _____

4. _____

5. _____

CHAPTER 6

Organizing Time and Managing Stress

*"Murphy's Three Laws:
It's not as easy as it looks.
It will take longer than you think.
If something can go wrong, it will."*

Welcome to the Big Time! •••••••

Today when you awoke to get ready for school, you discovered that the electricity went off during the night, and you're going to be late for your morning class, in which you have a mid-term examination. As you throw on your clothes and squirt toothpaste into your mouth because you can't take the time to fully brush your teeth, you hear the heavy clap of thunder and rain drops pounding on the roof of your house.

You drop your books in the stream of water pouring down your driveway as you run to your car. You near your exit from the expressway and hear a loud thump, your car swerves from side-to-side because you have a flat tire.

Thirty minutes later, you arrive on campus to find there's no place to park. You're late, it's raining, and you have a test. You say, "What the heck," and park on the grass anyway, knowing you'll find a ticket upon your return. You say a silent prayer that your instructor will allow you into class late to take the exam.

Does this sound unrealistic? Maybe not! Just talk to some of your classmates and hear some of their horror stories. Two of the more important lessons to learn in college are managing time and handling stress. The inability to practice good time management and to deal with stress can have a negative impact on your academic performance.

Time Management ••••••••••••

One of the most difficult things to learn is managing time. We are accustomed to having others set the agenda for what we do and when we do it. In addition, most of us give in to our preference for having fun and being entertained. Managing time effectively requires a discipline and commitment that are sometimes neither fun nor entertaining!

So, how can the typical student like you become a better time manager? A good starting point is to identify how, where, and when you use your time. It is helpful to begin by spending an entire week monitoring your time. That means writing down what you do, when you do it, and how long it takes. It also means being honest with yourself. Good time management requires acknowledging how you really spend time, not making up something that resembles a "wish list."

Try monitoring your time for the next week using Exercise 6.1. There are 24 hours in a day. How do you really make use of those hours?

Setting Priorities •••••••••••••

Now that you have some idea of how you spend your time in a typical week, a second consideration in time management is establishing weekly priorities to help guide your decisions about use of time. What are the most important things in your life? Are you spending your time accordingly? Are there obligations that compete for your time, for example, work and school? Personal interests and home responsibilities? Studying and social time?

Outlining a list of priorities for the next week using Exercise 6.2 will provide a framework in which to analyze where you can make changes. You may not have thought about priorities or that, indeed, they influence what you choose to do and how you make use of your time. We all have some things we **have to do** and some things we **want to do.** Identifying priorities involves writing down the "have to" and the "want to" items, whatever they may be.

Consider for a few minutes what is necessary or required of you from day-to-day for the next week. Also consider whether this is an ongoing commitment (taking my brother to school in the morning, going to my job, going to classes) or a one-time commitment (writing a paper for English class, preparing for a test, attending a friend's birthday party). What are your priorities for this next week?

Now think about some things that you would **like** to do this week if you have time. Would you like to watch a new video? Wash the car? Play tennis with a friend? Add these items to the second list. These items should not be as important as those on the first list and represent a "wish list" if time permits. Check your two lists to see if you want to move something from one list to the other.

Using a Priority List •••••••••••••

Let's use these two lists, the things you **must do** and the things you would **like to do,** to create a final list using Exercise 6.3 which represents your time priorities for the next week. Remember, this list does not include the routines that also require your time each day or most days (sleeping, eating, and so forth).

Now you have a complete list of everything you need to do in the next week. Knowing *what you need to do* is the first step in taking charge of your time. There are 168 hours in the week. Now you have all the information you need to plan how you will use them. Use them wisely and you will never say, "I don't have enough time."

General Principles of Time Management • • • • • • • • • •

Now that you are thinking about how you would like to spend time and what priorities may directly or indirectly influence the choices you make, let's think about some other established principles of time management that may help you with future decisions.

- **Making A Personal Commitment:** Good time management requires personal commitment. Once you decide what you need to do to use your time wisely, you need to be willing to act on that information. Nothing will change if you don't make changes. Students often try to use time management strategies that don't work for them; as a result, they become frustrated and give up.
- **Finding the Best Strategy:** Picking a time management strategy that will work for you is an important part of success. Some students like to create a detailed weekly schedule; others prefer an outline with some flexibility. Some students use an appointment book or planner; others make a daily list of "things to do." Selecting from among all the options is an important step.
- **Recognizing Your Needs:** The best strategy in the world won't work for you if you fail to recognize your needs. If you must work a significant number of hours each week in order to pay for school, it may be necessary to carry fewer credits or not participate in that club or organization that interests you. What is most important to accomplish? Once you recognize your needs, you can set realistic priorities.
- **Establishing Priorities:** Earlier we talked about the importance of identifying things in your life that are important. These priorities are linked to your needs and help you to determine how and when you will use your time. Most people have immediate or short-term priorities (this week) and distant or long-term priorities (this term or this year). Time management is generally related to those short-term, day-to-day decisions. Those short-term decisions and choices help determine whether or not longer-term goals are met.
- **Maintaining Flexibility:** While having a schedule is important, you should also recognize that sometimes the schedule cannot be maintained. Illness, an accident, or changed circumstances at home are all conditions which can and do disrupt the best-planned schedule. Often students believe they can "manage" without making changes. This inflexible thinking can lead to added stress. When there are major changes in your life circumstances, sometimes you must re-think both your short-term and long-term priorities.
- **Balancing Your Life:** School commitments, a part-time job, personal time for socializing and relaxing, and time for relationships, including family and friends, are all important dimensions to consider in planning how you will use your time. A major consideration should be balance. Too much time spent in any one area often leads to stress and tension.

These basic principles will assist you in developing a time management strategy tailor-made for your needs. This strategy will benefit you as a student and, eventually, in your life beyond college. Effective time managers are well organized and are usually able to fit in all of the various things they need to do or want to do.

You can avoid last-minute cramming sessions or all-nighters. You can have time to go to the movies, attend a party, or join your family for a special event. You can turn in papers on time, complete all of your assigned chapters for the week, and still find time to talk with a friend who has a problem.

A well-known time management expert, Alan Lakein, advocates what he calls the 80/20 rule. This "rule" says that 80 percent of the value in any set of activities comes from 20 percent of the identified activities. In other words, 80 percent of the benefits you want will come from only 20 percent of all the possible choices you've identified. While the percentages may vary, the concept is sound. Most of our time is spent on activities that produce fewer real benefits. The key, of course, is to know at any given moment what expenditures of time will benefit you most.

Look at the revised list of priorities you developed earlier. Now number the items on your list in order of importance. Which is the most important thing you need to do during this next week? Continue the process of renumbering until each item is in order, from most important (number one) to least important (number eight).

If the 80/20 theory holds true, and, if you have accurately identified what you need to do, you will benefit most by completing the first two items on the list. If time permits in the next week, you can continue to work down the list once the first two are accomplished.

Study Time •••••••••••••••

Some of the most inefficient use of time is found in students' study schedules. The most popular study strategies are some of the least effective. Let's review a few of these from a time management perspective.

- **Cramming:** Many students believe that cramming is a good way to pass a test. The problem is that cramming cannot replace real study time. While a last-minute review may provide some "instant re-call" of terminology or formulae, it does not sub-stitute for reading, reviewing, and, if necessary, memorizing. Time spent studying on a regular basis never can be replaced by cramming.
- **Long Study Sessions:** It is not unusual for students to plan their study time in blocks of two or more hours. In fact, shorter sessions are more effective. Research on retention of information suggests that after 45 to 60 minutes, the capacity to recall what is read or reviewed declines. Several shorter study ses-sions spaced throughout the day will produce better results for most students. Use that time between classes!
- **Studying Alone:** There is much to be gained from studying alone but more to be gained from form-ing a study group. Students who study together find that they learn more because each group member brings a different perspective to the sub-ject. By reviewing notes, discussing assigned read-ing, and providing some moral support, students in groups learn from each other and often fill in gaps in their materials from the class. Consider forming a study group for some or all of your classes, but remember, a study group is not a social group!
- **Studying With Friends:** This is the counterpoint to studying alone. Being with friends is fun. It is relaxing. It is a time to catch up on all that is hap-pening. It may not be the best way to study for academic success! While time with friends is enjoy-able, the question that must be answered is, "How much studying will be done?" Forming a study group with classmates is different from studying with friends.

The Weekly Schedule ••••••••••

A weekly schedule is helpful in planning for those activities and commitments that are ongoing. You might include the days and times of classes, work hours, and meeting commitments. You might also in-clude time needed for travel, leisure, and study.

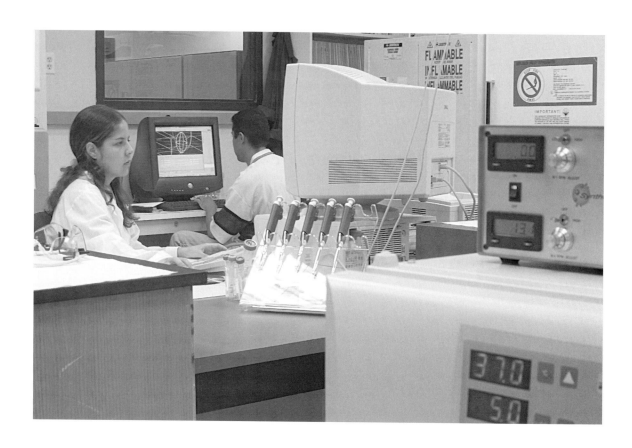

No matter how much detail goes into a weekly schedule, it is only a general guide. It helps you to see the larger time blocks required each day and provides a frame for developing a daily schedule or list of things to do.

Sample Schedule Analysis • • • • • • •

Our student, Peter Panther, is carrying 13 credits for Fall Term and is working at his part-time job 16 hours a week. On a typical day, Peter has two classes. Where possible, he has scheduled review/study time after each class to go over notes, look at the next reading assignments and homework, and plan for additional study time.

Peter has scheduled some exercise time (karate lessons two days a week) and a weekly library visit. If no assignments require library work, this becomes a planned study time. Peter also meets twice a week with a study group for his biology class. The group members usually bring their lunch to the meeting which is held in a group member's room in student housing.

Peter finds he usually needs, on the average, 12 hours a week for reading, homework, and projects. Sometimes he extends his review sessions in the mornings Monday through Thursday in order to work on class assignments. He also plans study time in the evening and on the weekends depending on what needs to be done each week. He finds that, with 10 hours a week of scheduled time, he does not need as much time at night and on weekends as his friends seem to need.

Peter finds he has time for active participation in one student organization. He has limited his involvements because he likes to have some time for hanging out with friends and participating in family activities.

The schedule allows Peter time for his main priorities (school and work) as well as his other activities (karate, a student organization, and family). It includes flexible unscheduled time which he can use on a daily basis as he chooses.

Planning a Day • • • • • • • • • • • • • • •

A typical daily schedule involves planning for a variety of tasks—studying, working, seeing friends, making phone calls, running errands. Sometimes the easiest way to plan for a week is to look at what needs to be done each day.

Daily schedules are usually more detailed than weekly schedules and reflect the specific tasks you plan to complete. A daily schedule also provides the detail missing from a weekly time plan. For most students, a well-conceived daily schedule is the most important tool in effective time management. Think about what you need to accomplish tomorrow and using the format in Exercise 6.4, identify all the things you **specifically** want to attempt to accomplish.

Each day, set aside some time to think about your schedule for the next day. What do you need to do? Who do you need to see? To call? As you make your list, your day will begin to take shape. You can **manage** your time rather than feel overwhelmed by the number and variety of tasks you face as a student.

Using a Planning Calendar • • • • • • •

Carry a daily calendar with you and use it as your planning guide. A calendar will help you to keep up with appointments, tests, assignments, your work schedule, and other important information. If you plan to keep your calendar with you, find one that is easy to carry in your pocket or a book bag.

Some students prefer to use note cards or Post-its to record their daily list of things to do from their master calendar. This list is easier to carry than a calendar and can also be used to record notes about future deadlines and assignments that can be transferred to your master calendar. Find a format that works for you.

Deciding to Be in Charge • • • • • • • •

There is no substitute for learning to manage time. During your college years (and after), there will always be more to do than there is time in which to do it. Busy people usually are the most organized because they have to be. Disorganized people often believe they have no control over their time and behave accordingly.

You need to decide how you want to be. The choice is yours. To use time effectively and efficiently requires commitment. If you master the skills of time management, you increase the probability of becoming a better student, a better employee, and a better friend.

Stress Is a Part of Life • • • • • • • • • •

Stress is a part of everyone's life. Most stress is healthy because it causes you to examine yourself and make important changes to your routine to relieve

Figure 6.1 Sample Weekly/Daily Schedule

Name: Peter Panther   **Section:** Fall

	Monday	Tuesday	Wednesday	Thursday	Friday	Saturday	Sunday
8:00	English	Sociology	English	Sociology	Biology Lab		
9:00	Review/ Study	Review/ Study	Review/ Study	Review/ Study	↓		
10:00	↓	↓	↓	↓	Review		
11:00	Study Group	Biology	Study Group	Biology			
12:00	↓	Lunch	↓	Lunch	Lunch	Work	Work
1:00		Work		Work	Library	↓	↓
2:00	Math		Math		↓		↓
3:00	Review		Review				
4:00		↓		↓		↓	
5:00	Karate		Karate				
6:00							
7:00							
8:00							
9:00							
10:00							
11:00							
12:00							
1:00							
6:00							
7:00							

pressure. Anything that makes you healthier and happier improves your ability to perform better in and out of the classroom. There are times when every student falls victim to stress, depending on how you handle stress, you may or may not be severely affected.

When things aren't going well in your life, you probably find yourself feeling the pressure. As was the case with the unfortunate student described in the opening section of this chapter, there are usually situations or events which serve as warning signs to alert you that stress is building. We've suggested to you throughout this course and this text that problems are a natural occurrence for everyone; the better prepared you are to address obstacles you face, the less stress you are likely to experience. Most of you follow a daily regimen that has become so routine you could almost do it blindfolded. Anytime you vary this routine, stress results. Although change is good, unplanned changes in your routine may catch you off-guard. It is far better for **you** to control possible stress by planning ahead and being prepared for the unexpected. Exercise 6.5 can assist you in analyzing what is stressful for you and how you typically respond to stress. It can also assist you in identifying some alternative ways to respond.

Exercising and Staying Fit •••••••

Staying physically and mentally alert seems like good advice to follow. But how does one do this in a typical hectic week? When your schedule becomes so hectic that you're constantly on the run, you probably find yourself eating junk food or you don't take time to eat at all. You are likely to feel hungry and become irritable. You are also more susceptible to stress.

If you are used to eating breakfast every morning, and then you decide to skip eating the day you have a big exam because you want to take the extra time to study, you may find your concentration affected by your growling stomach! Diet and exercise affect how you feel and how you respond.

Regular exercise is one of the best ways to relieve stress. Most college campuses have an abundance of exercise facilities and opportunities. Various health and physical exercise clubs and organizations exist on campus. You can do everything from aerobics, jogging, and swimming to racquetball, basketball, and tennis. Complete lists of available activities are available in offices like the Campus Life Department, the Athletics Department, and the Health Center.

Include some form of exercise as a regular part of your weekly routine. You'll be surprised how well (yet tired!) you feel once you're done. Exercising may eliminate much of the daily stress you feel, although you may still need to deal with its cause. Exercise both your mind and your body. Take a study break when you're cramming for a big test. Do something that is fun and then come back to your work.

It is easy to advise you to avoid stressful situations; yet, they inevitably will occur. Prior to taking an examination, a good way to rid your stomach of the butterflies and anxiety you feel is to take a deep breath and let it out slowly. Do this several times. This simple exercise will make you feel better and gets rid of some of the jitters! This is also a good practice to try prior to giving a speech or classroom

---

Stress Management Checklist

If you are having difficulty handling stress, here are a few important tips:

- Don't change your normal routine prior to examinations.
- Eat well!
- Exercise and stay fit.
- Avoid "cramming" for exams.
- Keep up with assignments.
- Seek assistance in dealing with problems. Utilize campus resources, including counseling center, academic support center, and the health center.
- Examine your routine and determine if changes are needed, including cutting back on work hours, studying more, and decreasing involvement in activities.
- Take study breaks.
- Reward yourself for jobs well done!

presentation. Taking the time to gather your thoughts may help avoid putting you into a stressful situation before you even get started on that speech or report.

Using Campus Resources ········

We've attempted to demonstrate that problems with time management and stress are a part of everyone's life. It's how we deal with various pressures and problems that determine our success or failure. The same can be said about stress. We are well aware that there will be times when stress builds and may become too much of a burden for you to carry. It is at this juncture that you should seek help. On most campuses, there is a counseling center that offers the services of trained and licensed professionals who work regularly with students needing assistance to deal with problems, stress, and other concerns. Don't wait until you can't handle the pressure. Make an appointment and discuss your situation with someone who will help you find solutions. Workshops on handling stress are also held regularly on campus, so watch for advertisements about these programs in the student newspaper and on bulletin boards. Make an effort to attend.

You've been juggling a heavy schedule, handling your regular routine, and attempting to avoid stress. You've succeeded, so now what do you do? Reward yourself!

Don't forget to thank yourself for doing a good job by going out and having fun. Go to a party, a movie, or your favorite restaurant. Buy that new compact disc you've wanted, or call that close friend long distance just to say hello. There certainly isn't anything wrong with you celebrating your successes (just don't overdo it!). This is another way of feeling good about yourself, and feeling good relieves stress and makes you healthier and happier. Try it. You'll see what we mean!

Signs of Stress* ···············

In thinking about tests, it is not uncommon to experience a high degree of anxiety. This anxiety is known as Test Anxiety. As you begin or continue your education, start classes, do assignments, and write papers, you may discover that:

- your stomach becomes upset
- your hands are sweaty

*From *College Survival Handbook* by David A. Hurwitz. Copyright © 1988 by Kendall/Hunt Publishing Company. Used with permission.

- you stop eating and begin to lose weight or
- you gorge yourself and gain weight
- you can't sleep at night
- you catch colds and flu
- you have constant headaches
- you become irritable
- you have trouble making decisions

You may ask yourself, "Is this what college is supposed to be? Did I spend all that money to be miserable? Why is this happening?" Anxiety or stress affects the body in many ways. You may not be experiencing all of those negative symptoms but you may have some. To find out why, you need to understand what is happening. Hopefully you came to college to learn. Learning is defined as, "A relatively permanent change in behavior as a result of experience." Stress can be defined as, "Your body's reaction to LEARNING!" You cannot eliminate the stress in your life, but you can learn to manage it more effectively and let it work for you rather than against you.

The Stress Reaction: How It Works* • • • • • • • • • • • • • • •

Stress is your body's reaction to change. According to Hans Selye, when you encounter a stressor, a change, your body will react through a series of stages called the General Adaption Syndrome, of GAS for short. Good changes or bad can be stressors, for example, trying to find a parking place on campus or winning the Lottery.

Stage 1. Alarm: You first notice the stressor (e.g., you are about to hit another car). Physiological changes occur in your body:

- Increase in adrenaline
- Increase in heart rate
- Increase in respiration
- Decrease in digestive actions (your stomach doesn't need to be working when you're trying to avoid hitting another car).

Stage 2. Resistance: You deal with the stressor (e.g., you hit the brakes, turn the wheel). Fight or Flight! All your resources, physical and mental, are available for you to use.

In normal daily circumstances, as you encounter stressors you move back and forth between the first two stages. When an intense stressor has been removed, or at the end of the day, you may feel exhausted or fatigued, having used much of your energy resources to deal with the stressors. (When the accident is over, you may get out of the car, shake, pass out, or vomit.)

If the stressor is intense or if it continues over a long period, or if many stressors build up over a long period, you may reach the third stage of the stress reaction.

Stage 3. Exhaustion: When this stage is reached, the edgy resources of the body have been depleted and the body begins to deteriorate. This stage can ultimately lead to death. Before death, however, severe stress can lead to heart disease, ulcers, colitis, and cancer.

After dealing with stressors our body needs time to recuperate. Most of our daily stressors are not as intense as a car accident, but if we do not do something regularly to allow our body to "recoup," the stress can build up to the point where it is intense.

What Are the Symptoms? • • • • • • •

- **Indecisive:** You can't make up your mind. "What should I wear today? What should I eat for dinner?"
- **Illness:** Adrenaline (see Alarm Stage) destroys white blood cells, your body's immune system. You become less resistant to illnesses such as colds, flu, etc. About the fourth or fifth week of a term, many students will miss classes because of stress-related illnesses.
- **Tired or fatigued:** Fatigue from stress is imagined; you usually have the energy to do what you want.
- **Accident prone:** You tend to fall more often, or become injured. Many car accidents occur immediately after a family argument.
- **Poor sleep habits, day-dreaming, bored, forgetful.**
- **Change in eating habits, loss of appetite, or overeating.**
- **Edgy or irritable:** You argue easily, and take it out on the wrong people or pets.

What Can I Do about It? • • • • • • • • •

To manage stress you can:

- Remove or avoid the stressor
- Learn positive self-talk

*Hans Selye, The Stress of Life (New York: McGraw-Hill Book Company Inc., 1956) pp. 31–33.

- Do a body inventory
- Relax
- Exercise
- Build positive patterns into your life

Avoidance: Removing the stressor is definitely a possible management strategy, especially if the stressor poses a danger to you. When primitive humans encountered a snake, they might have run or killed the snake, thereby removing the stressor. Some students perceive their courses as posing a danger and find that for them the best way to manage is avoiding the stress by skipping class or not doing assignments. They would rather be "safe" and "comfortable" than to expose themselves to the discomfort of personal growth. They know what happens when they do nothing and they are comfortable with it. They have fallen into a pattern of failing and they are good at it. To develop and grow and reach your potential as a person it is necessary to take risks, to change, and to learn. "NO PAIN, NO GAIN." The absence of stress is death. There are many living "dead" who, because of fear, avoid doing what they need to do to grow.

Self-Talk: The degree to which you react or "get stressed" depends in part on what you say to yourself about the stressor. One step in stress management is learning positive self-talk. What are you saying to yourself about a test, talking to your instructor, or meeting another student? Improving your self-talk can be challenging. Exercise 6.6 is a relaxation exercise you can use to begin changing your attitudes toward your courses. Practice steps 1–9 until you are comfortable with the relaxation process. Then do all seventeen steps. Have someone read the steps to you or record the steps onto a tape.

Body Inventory: Each night before going to sleep, make a mental inventory of your body to note where you feel tension or pain. The places that feel sore are where you are holding your stress. Focus your attention to relax these areas. A massage can also help.

Relaxation: Find time once or twice a day for approximately 15 to 30 minutes to relax. After bouncing between the stages of stress all day long, relaxation allows your body to return to normal. Examples of good exercises include: Positive imagery, Yoga meditation, zazen, or simply sitting in a quiet, darkened room, and focusing on your breathing. The positive imagery exercise above is an excellent way to relax.

Regular Exercise: Some of your tensions can be worked off through regular exercise. The exercise should be aerobic, exercising the heart and lungs. Examples include swimming, walking, running, bicycling, or aerobic dance. Exercise should be done at least every other day for approximately 15 to 30 minutes.

Patterns: Try to build patterns into your life. The more things you do on a regular basis, the easier it will be to deal with the changes when they do occur. The best way to manage stress is to develop good habits and patterns.

But what is meant by habits and patterns? When you dress, which sock do you put on first? Your left or right, it's always the same! When you brush your teeth, where does your toothbrush start? It's always the same spot! When you put on a coat, which arm goes in the sleeve first? It's always the same! These habits help you get through the day without thinking about every little move you make. Most of your patterns or habits are helpful, but some may actually be leading you toward failure or they may actually have caused you to fail in the past.

Do the following examples of poor patterns sound familiar? When you try to study, do you have trouble concentrating? Do you spend 3/4 of your study time preparing your study area and only 1/4 of your time studying? Have you ever said, "My teachers don't treat me fairly?" Do you schedule classes early even though you like to sleep in? When your alarm goes off, do you keep "snoozing" until you end up arriving late for classes or appointments? If some of these examples sound like you, then you may have "PROGRAMMED YOURSELF TO FAIL!" Programmed to fail means that the loops of your life, the patterns and habits that you use for your daily survival, contain "glitches" that lead to failure.

If you choose to adopt the study habits and patterns in this book, you can eliminate the "glitches" and move toward success. The key is understanding that YOU CHOOSE! We are quick to place blame outside of ourselves, but we must learn to accept responsibility for what we feel and do. WHO CONTROLS YOU? YOU DO!

"PATTERNS! Heck, you mean I have to follow a SCHEDULE? Not me! I like to be spontaneous. I can't live by a schedule!"

Does that sound like you? If so, remember about your socks, and brushing your teeth. You are already

Figure 6.2 Reducing Stress in Academic Situations*

If you have to give a presentation in class . . .	Know your topic well, but don't try to memorize your talk. Take a deep breath before you begin. Dress well so that you feel good about your appearance. Remember that the class is made up of individuals whom you could talk to easily on a one-to-one basis.
If you are taking a final exam . . .	Get to class a little early. Depending on your learning style, either look over your notes one more time or relax and talk to a classmate about something else. Bring adequate supplies—two sharpened pencils with erasers, a pen, a bluebook, a calculator, or whatever you will need. Know that you have studied as well as you could.
If you feel there is a personality conflict between you and the teacher . . .	Always be prepared for class by completing assignments carefully. Observe the interactions between the teacher and successful students; then base your behavior on the actions of these students. Try to analyze the problem and take steps to correct it.
If you have to write a term paper . . .	Choose your topic as soon as you can so you can begin thinking about it. Think of the term paper as a series of short, related assignments so you won't be overwhelmed by it. Set and observe deadlines for completing each of the short "assignments." Plan to finish early in case something else demands your attention just before the due date.

living by an unconscious schedule which may be detrimental to your academic success as well as your health.

You need to start looking at your present patterns. Determine which ones are helpful and which ones you know are bad but you don't change because they are habits; they have become comfortable. When someone says "Let's party," do you ever say "NO?"

Summary • • • • • • • • • • • • • • • • • •

Learning to take responsibility for what happens to you on a day-to-day basis is an important part of managing your time and your stress levels. There will always be things that you have no control over; however, you have a lot of control over how you respond.

There is an old saying: "We cannot change the direction of the wind but we can adjust our sails." Learning to manage the situations and circumstances you encounter is like adjusting your sails; little adjustments usually keep you on course and headed where you want to go. If you wait for a Force Five gale, no amount of adjusting will help much. The secret in both sailing and life is to know when and how to make the adjustments!

Name _____ Date _____

Exercise 6.1 Weekly/Daily Schedule

	Monday	Tuesday	Wednesday	Thursday	Friday	Saturday	Sunday
8:00							
9:00							
10:00							
11:00							
12:00							
1:00							
2:00							
3:00							
4:00							
5:00							
6:00							
7:00							
8:00							
9:00							
10:00							
11:00							
12:00							
1:00							
6:00							
7:00							

Name _____   Date_____

This week I **must** do the following things:

1. _____

2. _____

3. _____

4. _____

5. _____

This week I would also **like to** do these things if time permits:

1. _____

2. _____

3. _____

4. _____

5. _____

Name _____ Date_____

Exercise 6.3 My "TO DO LIST" for Next Week ··········

In the next week, it is very important to me that I do these things. The things I **absolutely must do** are marked with an asterisk (*).

1. _____

2. _____

3. _____

4. _____

5. _____

6. _____

7. _____

8. _____

Exercise 6.4 Daily Plan For _____

(Date)

Name: _____   Section _____

Jobs to Complete	Due Date	Priority	Completed?
1.			
2.			
3.			
4.			
5.			
6.			
7.			
8.			
9.			
10.			

Phone Calls to Make

1.			
2.			
3.			
4.			

Name _____ Date_____

Exercise 6.5 Analysis of Stress

One way to learn to deal constructively with stress is to analyze your own behavior in stressful situations. What is your normal reaction? Is there a better way to react? What might you do next time? Then if a similar situation occurs, you will be better prepared to deal with it. Use the form below to keep track of the frequency of your stressful situations, actions to each situation, and ways to avoid or manage such situations if they should occur again. Just writing down the circumstances relieves some of your tension, and you can use the list later in discussions with your family and friends. The first blocks are filled in as an example.

Date	Cause of Stress	Reaction to Stress	How to Avoid/Manage Next Time
2/27	Couldn't get computer program to run.	Got mad—wanted to drop the course. Couldn't sleep.	Get started earlier. Get help. Check out program more thoroughly.

From *Developing Power in Reading* by Roe and Ross. Copyright © 1993 by Kendall/Hunt Publishing Company. Used with permission.

CHAPTER 7

Managing Your Finances

*"That money talks
I'll not deny.
I heard it once:
It said 'Goodbye.'"*
–Richard Armour

The Buck Stops Here • • • • • • • • • •

Among the many lessons you can learn in college, one of the most important may be managing your finances. Financial planning consists of more than merely managing and investing money. It includes making all the pieces of your financial life fit together.

One of the major reasons students cite for going to college is to improve their economic standard. Students believe that getting a college degree will make them more competitive in the job market (i.e., a high paying job), resulting in improved socio-economic conditions for themselves and their families. Potential income and status are further enhanced as additional degrees, particularly professional degrees, are earned.

College students are often on their own for the first time in their lives and are faced with the daunting task of managing their finances, developing and keeping a budget, and balancing a checkbook. Budgeting your financial resources is important in maintaining a reasonable standard of living. If you never have enough money, it can be quite frustrating. This is a good time to learn to develop a budget that shows your income and expenses so that you don't find yourself short of cash, in debt, and unable to pay your bills. You also need to develop a plan for financing your education so that you don't encounter unexpected financial problems which may cause you to withdraw from the university.

Many people with responsible jobs live paycheck to paycheck and rarely save any money. To avoid this situation, sound financial planning is advised. Why not start now? Learning to manage your finances is important so that when you graduate, you will already know how to budget properly and will be a step ahead of many other new professionals entering the work force.

Developing a Budget • • • • • • • • •

The best place to start is preparing a budget plan which you can follow for a month. Exercise 7.1 will assist you in this process. Know how much money you have coming in from all sources (income) for a month, and be familiar with your fixed and anticipated expenses. Fixed expenses are items such as rent, your car payment, insurance, food, and gasoline for commuting to campus. Anticipated expenses include entertainment, new clothing, and purchases like a beeper or a cellular phone.

A good budget plan will include allocating some money to open a savings account or to invest. A "nest egg" could come in handy in an emergency situation when unexpected and unavoidable expenses arise. In these situations, you can use your savings to make payments instead of drawing from money needed for your ongoing monthly expenses.

A key item in developing a budget is accepting that you will have to monitor and probably reduce your spending. Monthly budgets that end in the "red" aren't allowed! If you don't want to decrease your level of spending, then you must find ways to increase your income.

Learning to manage your money and get more out of it is not only easy, it is fun as well. Items to consider in developing an understanding of your financial circumstances and financial management needs include knowledge of checking accounts and credit cards, paying bills on time, employment, savings and investments, and buying wisely.

Checking Accounts • • • • • • • • • • • •

Banks are as different as their names and have different ways of serving their customers. When you open a checking account, shop around for the best deal. Don't forget to check on the services offered at other financial institutions including credit unions and savings and loan organizations. Financial companies are very competitive and offer varying deals to attract customers.

Once you have selected a bank and opened a checking account, set up your checkbook. Be sure to keep your checkbook balanced by adding all deposits and subtracting expenses as you write checks. Don't wait until your monthly bank statement arrives to learn that your account balance has dwindled to little or nothing!

Does your bank cover overdrawn checks? Most banks do not unless you have savings to cover the amount in question. "Bounced checks" are likely to result in charges from both your bank and the business which accepted your check. The business may turn you over to a collection agency to recover their money if the amount of the check was large. Bouncing checks can also affect your credit rating. When you attempt to make a major purchase such as a car or house, or even apply for a credit card, a bad credit rating could result in you not getting approved.

Items to Consider When You Compare Banks:

- Do they offer free checking?
- Are there monthly service fees?
- Do they cover your account when you overdraw, and if so, what fee do they charge?
- Do they offer an ATM card, and if so, is there a monthly service fee?
- If they provide an ATM card, are you charged a fee each time you use the card (not only at the bank that issued the card but at other ATM machines as well)?
- Do you have to maintain a monthly minimum balance, and if you don't, what is the penalty fee?
- What are the hidden fees the bank may charge for the "privilege" of having your business?

Once your monthly bank statement arrives, be sure to reconcile your account to the proper balance. This means reviewing every item on the bank statement and matching it against every item in your checkbook. Even if you're a penny off, accept the challenge of locating the mistake and correcting it. You'll actually feel good about it once you're done, although the exercise may sometimes be frustrating and time consuming.

Credit Cards • • • • • • • • • • • • • • • • •

Credit card debt is at the highest level it has ever been in this country. The average debt on major credit cards among consumers between the ages of 20 and 30 years old has nearly tripled since 1990. If you don't want to become part of that statistic, be wary of credit cards. College students are easy targets for companies that use promotional gimmicks to get you to apply for their cards.

Cards are easy to obtain and you get a "free" t-shirt or a coffee mug besides! Did you ever ask yourself why credit card companies are so anxious to have your business? The answer is simple: college students are more likely than many other segments of the population to **use** their credit cards. College students, you included, frequently have limited financial resources coupled with a strong consumer instinct. Students like to buy things. Without cash, the easiest way to make a purchase is with a credit card!

There are good and bad reasons for having credit cards. Two good reasons are that they are safer to carry than huge amounts of cash when making purchases, and they enable you to establish a credit history. On the flip side, however, credit cards are easy to use, and you may find that you've made too many purchases, resulting in large balances and heavy debt. Once your balances grow too large, meeting the minimum payments becomes difficult. At this point, many students begin working extra hours, cutting classes, and may even drop out of school or find they are dismissed because of poor grades.

A word to the wise: if you can't live without one, have one major credit card and pay off your balance each time you receive your bill. The average balance for a college student's credit card is $2,400! The interest rate on some cards is higher than the minimum payment. Some people find it impossible to pay off their balances because interest rates are so high. Remember that interest starts accumulating immediately for new purchases when you carry forward a previous balance. It is also important that you become familiar with the grace period that your credit card company allows for payments.

If you find that you are in credit card debt, discuss the situation with your financial institution and arrange payments that meet your budget. The company may not be pleased with this course of action, but they'd rather have some payment than none at all, and they certainly don't want you to file for bankruptcy.

Bankruptcy should be the last resort for anyone to take, particularly for a college student. In 1996, approximately one million people filed for personal bankruptcy in the United States. For the rest of your life, filing for bankruptcy could return to haunt you when you attempt to make major purchases or receive credit. Seek credit counseling before you take this drastic step!

If you believe that you absolutely need a credit card, go ahead and get one, but be honest with yourself about why you want that little piece of plastic. If you manage well with paying cash or writing checks for your purchases, stay away from credit cards for the present.

Items To Consider in Choosing A Credit Card:

- Shop around for the best deal, including the lowest interest charged. Some cards have an annual fee and some do not.
- Why pay an annual fee if you don't have to? The credit card companies are competitive, and you can often negotiate better deals with banks or credit unions than those used in their advertisements.
- Consider getting a credit card that is also an ATM or a debit card; your purchases will be automatically deducted from your checking or savings account. (Be sure to write these cash charges down and keep your balances current and accurate.)

Pay Bills on Time

College students accumulate many types of bills, including credit card charges, college tuition and book costs, cellular phones and beepers, car loans, and if you live in an apartment instead of home, rent, utility, and phone payments. Be sure to include all of your monthly expenses in the budget that you develop.

Most monthly bills list the minimum payment due as well as the payment due date. If you miss the payment deadline, late charges are applied. You'll also be penalized if you don't make the minimum payment. Always try to pay the full balance of each bill or pay more than the minimum amount due (if you can't pay the balance). This will help you avoid those late charges or interest payments.

Be aware that late payments may also affect your credit rating. Credit card companies and banks where you have loans often report consistent late payments or other payment problems to their credit agencies. This is why it is important to make payments on time or discuss your payment problems with your financial institution.

Increasing Your Income

There are various ways for you to increase your income to assist you in meeting ongoing expenses and avoiding debt. Foremost among the recommendations is a part-time job. Before you commit to a job, make sure that you weigh carefully the demands of working. Be sure it doesn't interfere with your real reason for being here: academics. Many students find it necessary to work in order to attend college. Successful students recognize that the emphasis must remain on attending classes and allowing adequate study time.

Many students find it more beneficial and enjoyable to work on campus rather than in the community. Various jobs are available throughout campus. These positions can be found through personal contacts or through postings in the university's Personnel Office, Financial Aid Office, or Career Services Office. Some students are eligible for College Work Study positions. These campus jobs are funded by both the Federal Government and the university and are awarded as a part of a financial aid award through the Financial Aid Office.

For positions off campus, students can use personal contacts, including family, family friends, and former employers, apply in person at various businesses, or visit the university's Career Services Office to peruse listings for part-time employment.

Remember that the purpose of working part-time is to earn money while you're getting an education. A part-time job should **never** interfere with your education.

Key Items to Remember:

- Pay bills on time!
- Pay the full balance if possible, and if not, pay the minimum amount due.
- If you have trouble making payments, discuss your situation with your financial institution.
- Seek credit counseling.

Another way to increase your income is borrowing money; however, this raises your debt and requires repayment. A large purchase, a car for example, may require that you borrow money. The monthly payment for the loan must be added to your budget expenses.

Investments or interest on savings or other accounts represent an additional source of income. If your financial situation allows you to begin making personal investments in stocks, mutual funds, or long-term savings plans, be sure to get good advice and become an educated consumer. This will enable you to begin making sound investments now and hopefully receive a good return on your money for years to come.

Additional monies may also be available through financial aid, scholarships, or other grants, if you are eligible. Applications as well as information for various forms of aid and assistance are available in the Financial Aid Office. You can also check with the librarian at the Reference Desk in the Library who can direct you to more information regarding various scholarships and grants. Other forms of aid are available through scholarships awarded by community or social agencies. Information can be located through a Web search or Financial Aid. Be careful to read all eligibility and other documentation carefully and meet application deadlines.

Key Items to Remember:

- Consider a part-time job to increase your income, but make sure your part-time job doesn't interfere with academics.
- Look for a part-time job on campus.
- Check your eligibility for the College Work Study Program in the Financial Aid Office.
- Apply for financial aid, scholarships, or grants to increase your income.
- If your finances permit, consider investments and other savings programs.

Shop Wisely

Comparison shopping is another way to save your money. Wouldn't you visit several car dealerships if you are going to buy a new car so that you can get the best deal and save money? You should do the same with smaller purchases. Look for bargains and wait for sales. Some businesses will even negotiate the price of high-ticket items such as audio equipment, phones, and clothing because these items typically have a high price mark-up.

Sometimes it is better to pay a little more for a better quality item than to save some money on something that will not last as long. In the long run, you can save money by purchasing a better product because the cheaper item is more likely to require repairs or need replacement sooner.

It is a good practice to pay cash for your purchases. If you charge small items, you will probably make interest and finance payments if you don't pay the balance when you receive your bill. That means you will pay more for the charged merchandise. Keep the receipts for your purchases in case there is a question about your bill or you need to return them. Some stores will not allow exchanges or refunds without a receipt.

Another way to save on purchases is to use coupons or take advantage of store promotions. If you plan to make a major purchase, ask the store management when the item may go on sale. If you can wait until the sale, you will save money. When making large purchases, examine your budget first and determine whether or not you can afford the purchase. If the expenditure puts you in a situation where your expenses exceed your income, delay the purchase. You could even begin a small weekly or monthly savings plan to cover expenses associated with a large purchase.

Getting Out of Debt

You say that you've tried everything and you still can't get out of debt? There is always a solution! Here are a few recommendations frequently suggested by the "experts" on money and debt management:

- Use savings or cash to reduce or eliminate debt, but do not exhaust your entire savings in case you have a severe emergency and need immediate cash.

Key Items to Remember:

- Comparison shop, look for bargains, and negotiate.
- Pay cash for purchases.
- Keep receipts for purchases.
- Wait for sales.
- Use coupons and other promotions.
- Buy quality items.

- Comparison shop for banks that offer better checking and ATM options and switch your account.
- Locate a better credit card deal and transfer your balances to the lower interest card.
- Cut up and discard the credit cards once the balances are transferred to the new card.
- Carry only one credit card and don't use it unless absolutely necessary!
- Seek credit counseling. Various resources are available in the community which offer advice on managing finances and debt.

- Check the Yellow Pages or contact the State Consumer Protection Agency or local Chamber of Commerce for consumer counseling recommendations. At the university, you can check with the Financial Aid Office or Counseling and Psychological Services for community referrals.

Filing for bankruptcy should be your last resort. Remember that this course of action remains a part of your credit history forever and may have a negative impact on your future financial transactions.

Summary

Most individuals work about 40 years in the course of their lifetime. At an annual average salary of $30,000, that means the "average" person will make more than $1,000,000 in his or her career. How will you spend all of that money?

Efficient and proper financial planning and management reduces stress and enables individuals to enjoy a better quality of life. Developing and following a budget, being knowledgeable about sound financial management, and learning and understanding the technicalities of finances can be invaluable for you in college and for the rest of your life.

Exercise 7.1 Monthly Budget

MONTH ——————-

INCOME

Source		Amount
1. _____	$ _____
2. _____	$ _____
3. _____	$ _____
4. _____	$ _____
5. _____	$ _____
TOTAL:	$ _____

FIXED EXPENSES

Type		Amount
1. _____	$ _____
2. _____	$ _____
3. _____	$ _____
4. _____	$ _____
5. _____	$ _____
6. _____	$ _____

ANTICIPATED EXPENSES:

7. _____	$ _____
8. _____	$ _____
9. _____	$ _____
10. _____	$ _____
TOTAL:	$ _____

TOTAL INCOME: $ _____

TOTAL EXPENSES: $ _____

Subtract expenses from income

BALANCE (Savings): $ _____   (Balance *must* be positive!)

Exercise 7.2 Developing a Budget

Your task in this exercise is to develop a budget for Sean, one of your classmates. This exercise can be done individually or in small groups. Each group should select a spokesperson to present the group's budget to the class. The time limit is twenty minutes.

The following are Sean's financial conditions for each month:

A place to live. He doesn't like roommates.

Three meals a day.

He has an old car that is paid for and gets 12 miles per gallon.

His car insurance is $80 per month.

He works 25 hours per week at $6.00 per hour. He gets paid every Friday. The Social Security deduction is 7.51%.

He has a school loan payment of $50 per month.

He likes to party.

He belongs to a health club. Dues are $50 per month.

He goes out to eat at least three times per week.

His girlfriend goes to school 500 miles away. He calls her twice a week.

His job is 10 miles from school. He lives midway between school and work.

His mom and dad give him money about every three months, usually $150 to $200.

He has two credit cards with a combined balance of $300.

He goes to a sporting event or a movie about once every two weeks.

CHAPTER 8

Maintaining a Healthy Lifestyle

*"All the things I really like to do are
either illegal, immoral, or fattening."*
—Alexander Woollcott

Healthy Lifestyles through Wellness • • • • • • • • • • • •

HOW ARE YOU? You probably answered "fine" without really thinking. But, how do you **really** feel . . . about yourself, your life, your family and friends, your lifestyle, your health? Chances are that you may not have considered all of the many facets that constitute your true well-being. Do you eat well? Do you exercise regularly? Do you smoke or drink? Do you have close friends with whom you can share your experiences, both good and traumatic? Are you under extreme stress to get good grades, perform well on the job, or be a good parent? Do you get regular medical checkups and do you practice self-care? Are you aware of safety and environmental factors that contribute to your health? This chapter will address some of these complex questions and help you develop important strategies that will enable you to live life to the fullest, both physically and emotionally.

Traditionally, health was simply defined as the absence of disease or symptoms. This concept has gradually evolved over the past 50 years so that health is now defined by the World Health Organization as a continuous and harmonious balance of physical, mental, spiritual, intellectual, and social well-being. This continuum of a "balanced," healthy lifestyle has been defined as **wellness.** True wellness entails forming a contract with yourself to engage in healthy behaviors and attitudes that enhance the quality of your life and personal performance.

To achieve this state of wellness, you must maintain a balance of six continually changing dimensions that affect your overall health. These components of wellness are:

1) Physical—the ability to maintain positive lifestyle habits to enable you to perform your daily tasks. Such components of the physical dimension of wellness entail eating healthy foods, maintaining appropriate weight and body fat, performing regular exercise to maintain cardiovascular fitness, and avoiding the abuse of tobacco, alcohol, and other drugs.

2) Emotional—the ability to manage stress and express your emotions appropriately by recognizing and accepting your feelings about the events of your life. Stress is part of everyone's life, but your ability to properly manage life's stressful events can greatly influence your overall health potential.

3) Spiritual—the belief in an abstract strength that unites all of your internal energies. This strength can include religion and/or nature, but also includes your values, ethics, and morals. Your personal sense of spirituality provides meaning and direction to your life, enabling you to learn, develop, and meet new challenges successfully.

4) Social—the skill to interact successfully with other people at work, school, and in the community. This dimension of wellness encompasses your ability to handle relationships, both intimate and casual.

5) Intellectual—the ability to learn and use your knowledge effectively to enhance your overall health. Knowledge of self-care techniques, disease risk factors, as well as your family history of disease, are all important components to achieving intellectual wellness.

6) Environmental—the physical and social setting that influences your lifestyle. This dimension includes your personal safety practices, such as wearing seat belts, to your efforts to help promote a clean environment.

These six dimensions of wellness overlap and components of one often can directly or indirectly affect factors in another. Some health parameters are under your direct control and some are not. For example, your lifestyle behaviors (diet, exercise, habits) constitute the greatest percentage of life's influences on the quality of your life.

Relationships involving family, friends, and the community are also important, as are factors pertaining to the quality of health care you receive by physicians and health care facilities. Approximately 85 percent of the factors influencing your health are within your control. The remaining 15 percent are beyond your individual control and consist of heredity predispositions. However, if your medical history reveals a family tendency toward a specific disease, such as heart disease or cancer, your lifestyle decisions can delay the onset, minimize the disease's effects, or possibly even prevent the disease from occurring. This is why a good knowledge of preventive medicine becomes so important.

This chapter was written by Robert Dollinger, M.D., Executive Director of University Health Services at Florida International University. It is used by permission of the author.

Health Benefits of Wellness • • • • •

You can achieve wellness through improving your knowledge about health, eliminating risk factors from your lifestyle, practicing good self-care habits and preventive medicine by having periodic medical check-ups, and maintaining a positive attitude. Some of the benefits of wellness include:

- a decreased risk of developing chronic diseases;
- a decreased risk of accidents;
- a decreased recovery time after injury and illness;

- an improved cardiovascular system function (heart efficiency and blood vessel diameter both increase);
- an increase in muscle tone, strength, and flexibility;
- an improved physical appearance—less fat, greater muscle tone;
- an increased ability to manage stress and resist depression;
- proper nutrition for optimal growth, repair, immune function, and development;
- a higher self-esteem;
- an increase in energy level, productivity, and creativity; and
- an improved awareness of your personal needs and the ways to achieve them.

Wellness as a Challenge • • • • • • • • •

Your belief in your ability to perform healthy behaviors will influence your actual choices, your degree of effort to make the change, your persistence, and your emotional reactions to the new lifestyle. Your ability to turn your health-related goals into reality is dependent on formulating a plan of action. This lifestyle modification has several steps:

1) Evaluate your personal health habits.
Make a list of your behaviors that promote health and make another list of your behaviors that are harmful. Once you have compiled both of your lists, note which behaviors present the greatest threat to your overall well-being. These behaviors should be targeted for change first.

2) Set realistic, specific, observable, and measurable goals.
Don't expect miracles. Setting goals that are too ambitious often ensures failure. Frequently, the fear of failure may discourage future efforts. View the lifestyle change as a lifetime change, not simply temporary. Strive for moderation at first rather than striving for complete behavior reversal or abstinence. Behavior changes that are "slow-but-steady" are the ones most likely to result in permanent success.

3) Formulate a strategy for success.
Most people want to make positive changes but too often find reasons why they cannot make changes. They may not have the time, are too tired, or simply feel embarrassed. What are some of your reasons? From time to time, we all have them. These barriers to change must be avoided if you are to achieve your healthy goals.

4) Evaluate your progress.
How well are you doing? The only way to consistently stick with your new healthy behavior is to receive feedback by monitoring your progress. This feedback evaluation allows you to modify the program, enabling you to better achieve your goals. Initially, the evaluation periods should take place relatively frequently, such as daily or weekly. After periods of consistent success, the time interval between evaluation sessions could be lengthened to monthly.

Success does not have to be all-or-none. This manner of thinking can be detrimental to your overall motivation to change. When your goals are not fully realized, simply reshape your goals, set a more realistic time schedule, or formulate different intervention strategies, and **TRY AGAIN**. More importantly, answer these questions:

"What did I learn from this experience?"

"What can I do differently?"

Based on your answers, make a new contract and begin immediately. Remember that lifestyle change is never easy but its rewards will last a lifetime.

Healthy Nutrition: You Are What You Eat • • • • • • • • • • • • • • • •

Our dietary habits play a key role in both how long we live and how well we feel. A healthy diet is one that features a proper variety and balance of foods to supply our body with nutrients and essential dietary factors required for growth, energy, and repair. There are six nutrients: proteins, carbohydrates, fats, vitamins, minerals, and water. **Protein** is necessary for growth and repair, forming the basic building blocks of muscles, bones, hair, and blood. Meat, poultry, fish, eggs, milk, cheese, dry beans, and nuts are excellent dietary sources of protein.

Carbohydrates provide the body with glucose, its basic fuel. There are two types of carbohydrates: simple and complex. Simple carbohydrates are sugars, which are responsible for providing short bursts of energy. Examples of dietary sugars include glucose, sucrose (table sugar), fructose (the sugar found in fruits), honey, and syrup. Complex carbohydrates consist of starches and fiber, important ingredients of cereals, breads, rice, pasta, fruits, and vegetables. Soluble fiber, found in oats, beans, apples, and citrus fruit, has been shown to lower blood cholesterol levels and decrease the risk of heart disease.

Fats are high calorie nutrients that come in two primary types: saturated and unsaturated. Saturated fats, found in animal products such red meat, egg yolk, and butter, have been shown to increase the blood cholesterol levels and increase the risk of heart disease. In contrast, monounsaturated and polyunsaturated fats are found primarily in foods of plant origin and have been shown to lower blood cholesterol levels. Polyunsaturated fats are found in safflower and corn oils whereas canola and olive oil are monounsaturated fats. In contrast to protein and carbohydrates which contain four calories per gram, fat contributes nine calories per gram when metabolized in the body. For this reason, a simple way to lose weight is to decrease the amount of dietary fat.

Figure 8.1 Wellness Strategies for Top Performance: Academically and Athletically

Exercise:

- Do aerobic exercises (walking, jogging, swimming, cycling, etc.) for 30 minutes three to four times a week.
- Incorporate exercise into your daily activities (e.g., take the stairs)
- Always do warm-up and cool-down exercises and stretch before and after your aerobic session to improve flexibility and decrease risk of injury.

Nutrition:

- Eat foods high in complex carbohydrates (breads, cereals, fruits, vegetables, pasta) to constitute 48% of your total daily calories
- Limit simple sugars (table sugar, soft drinks, candy); consume only with meals.
- Limit saturated fat intake (animal fats, whole milk, etc.); consume more fat calories as monounsaturated (canola and olive oil) and polyunsaturated (vegetable oils) fats.
- Drink at least eight glasses of water daily.

Stress management:

- Improve your time management and organizational skills (set priorities, don't procrastinate, make a daily schedule with flexible time and follow it).
- Practice progressive muscle relaxation, meditation, yoga, and deep-breathing exercises.

Self-care:

- Don't smoke.
- Only drink alcohol responsibly; (e.g. don't drink and drive, no more than two or three drinks in one sitting, etc.)
- Perform breast or testicular self-exams monthly.
- Have regular medical screenings and physical exams.
- Know your blood pressure and cholesterol numbers.
- Practice abstinence or safer sex (always use condoms).
- Sleep at least seven to eight hours daily and develop a regular sleep-wake cycle.
- Read about current health topics and medical discoveries; check the Internet.

Safety:

- Always wear a seat belt.
- Learn cardiopulmonary resuscitation (CPR).
- Check smoke detectors in your home annually.

Figure 8.2 A Sample Contract for Lifestyle Change

I, _____, pledge that I will accomplish the goals listed below.

- **Personal Goal:** Improve my fitness level

- **Motivating Factors:** I want to have more energy and feel better.

- **Change(s) I Promise to Make to Reach This Goal:** Jog for 20–30 minutes at least three times a week.

- **Start Date:** January 1

- **Intervention Strategies:**
  1. I will walk early in the morning before classes.
  2. I will walk after classes on days when it is raining in the morning.

- **Plan for Making This Change:**
  1. First week: walk for 10 minutes three times a week.
  2. Weeks 2 to 4: Increase the amount of walking time by five minutes every week until I walk for 20–30 minutes each session.
  3. Week 5: Evaluate my progress.
  4. Weeks 5 to 9: Gradually increase my speed.
  5. Week 10: Evaluate my progress.
  6. After the first 10 weeks: Continue my morning jogs three times a week.

- **Target Date for Reaching Goal:** March 15

- **Reward for Reaching Goal:** Buy a new, expensive pair of jogging shoes.

- **If I Need Help:** I can call my friend _____ to walk or jog with me.

Signed: _____

Witness: _____

Date: _____

Vitamins are organic nutrients which work with the body's enzymes to enable biochemical reactions to take place. Vitamins C and E, as well as beta-carotene, serve as antioxidants, substances that protect cells from dangerous free radicals produced by normal metabolic processes. Antioxidants have been shown to reduce the incidence of heart disease and certain types of cancer.

Minerals are inorganic substances found in food that are also essential for proper metabolism. Macrominerals (sodium, potassium, calcium, phosphorus, and magnesium) are required in larger amounts than are the trace minerals (iron, zinc, selenium, iodine, chromium, and fluoride). Calcium is the most abundant mineral in the body, responsible for bone integrity and prevention of osteoporosis, as well as for conduction of nerve impulses and cardiac contraction.

Approximately 60% of your weight consists of **water.** Water helps to digest foods, maintains proper body temperature, lubricates joints, and eliminates the body's waste products via urine. Water is necessary for survival, as we would die after only a few days without water. In contrast, we could survive for several weeks without food. You should drink at least eight glasses of water a day, not counting alcohol and drinks that contain the diuretic caffeine, such as coffee, tea, and certain soft drinks.

How Much Should I Eat? • • • • • • • •

According to the American Dietetic Association, 12% of your daily calories should come from protein; 58% from carbohydrates (of which 48% should be complex carbohydrates and only 10% simple sugars); and a total of 30% from fats (8% saturated fats, 12% monounsaturated fats, and 10% polyunsaturated fats). In contrast, the typical American diet consists of too much saturated fats and simple sugars and lacks sufficient amounts of complex carbohydrates. To best help you determine what your daily nutrient intake is, you need to understand the food pyramid.

The Food Guide Pyramid ········

In 1992, the United States Department of Agriculture published the Food Guide Pyramid, a new guideline to simplify the selections of foods that constitute a healthy diet. As shown in Figure 8.3, the Food Guide Pyramid incorporates five food groups plus fats, oils, and sugars. Foods in one category cannot replace those from another.

The foods at the base of the Food Pyramid form the foundation of a healthy diet and consist of foods high in complex carbohydrates—breads, cereals, rice, and pasta. The foods at the Pyramid's base are high in fiber, iron, protein, and B vitamins and should be consumed in the largest quantities, namely six to eleven servings daily. The second tier of the Food Pyramid consists of vegetables and fruits—foods that are high in fiber, low in fat, and high in vitamins A and C. Scientific studies have revealed that vegetables and fruits may prevent cancers of the lung, colon, stomach, bladder, and breast. According to the Food Pyramid, three to five servings of vegetables and two to four servings of fruits are recommended daily. Foods in the "Milk, Yogurt, and Cheese" group are high in calcium, protein, and vitamins A and B-12. Two servings per day are recommended. Foods in the "Meat, Poultry, Fish, Dry Beans, Eggs, and Nuts" group are excellent sources of protein, iron, zinc, phosphorus, and B vitamins. These foods are also high in fats and cholesterol and thus, you should choose low-fat varieties. Finally, foods at the apex of the Food Pyramid (the smallest part of the Pyramid) should be consumed in very small quantities. Fats, oils, and sweets are high in calories but supply little or no vitamins or minerals. Select foods from this category that are high in monounsaturated fats, such as canola or olive oils.

Using Campus Resources To Help You Eat Right ···········

Visit the campus Student Health Center, a primary care physician, or a registered dietician to receive a personal nutrition consultation. A licensed health professional can help you lose weight or gain weight; prescribe a diet to help control blood pressure, diabetes, or high cholesterol; or provide guidance concerning dietary supplements. Many campuses also offer wellness programs that provide personalized nutrition counseling as well as computerized diet assessments where you determine your caloric intake as well as the amount of fat, cholesterol, protein, fiber, sugar, sodium, calcium, and other nutrients.

Responsible Drinking ···········

The abuse of alcohol is the number one problem facing college students today. Although more students are choosing to abstain, approximately 85 percent of college students use alcohol. A small percentage of these students drink irresponsibly, either "high-risk" binge drinking (drinking five or more drinks at one sitting), drinking while under the legal drinking age, or driving under the influence of alcohol. The leading cause of death among college students is alcohol-related automobile accidents. The use and abuse of alcohol is also associated with most cases of campus violence, arrests, vandalism, rape, accidents, homicides, unwanted sex, sexually transmitted diseases and HIV/AIDS, unwanted pregnancies, poor grades, and drop-outs.

Alcohol can also impair your judgment. You may actually have sex with someone that you would normally not even go out to lunch with! However, the consequences of your decision, such as an unintended pregnancy, a sexually transmitted disease, or an accident resulting in a lifelong disability or death of a close friend, may last a lifetime.

Ethyl alcohol, or ethanol, is the type of alcohol found in alcoholic beverages. By definition, any drink containing 0.5% or more ethyl alcohol by volume is an alcoholic beverage. However, different drinks contain different amounts of alcohol. For example, one drink is defined as any of the following:

- one 12 oz can of beer (5% alcohol);
- one 4 oz glass of wine (12% alcohol); or
- one shot (1 oz) of distilled spirits, such as whiskey, vodka, or rum (50% alcohol). The alcohol content is expressed as **proof,** a number that is twice the percentage of alcohol: 80-proof gin is 40% alcohol, etc.

To determine the amount that you can safely drink, you need to determine the blood-alcohol concentration (BAC), the percentage of alcohol in the blood. The BAC is usually measured from your breath. Most people reach a BAC of 0.05% after consuming one or two drinks; at this level, they do not feel intoxicated. If they continue to drink past this BAC level, they start to feel worse, with decreased reaction times, slurred speech, and loss of balance and emotional control. The legal BAC in most states is 0.08%. Persons driving a motor vehicle with a BAC of 0.08% or greater are cited for driving under the influence and are subject to severe legal penalties and fines. At a BAC of 0.2%, a person is likely to pass out

Figure 8.3 Food Guide Pyramid

Food Guide Pyramid
A Guide to Daily Food Choices

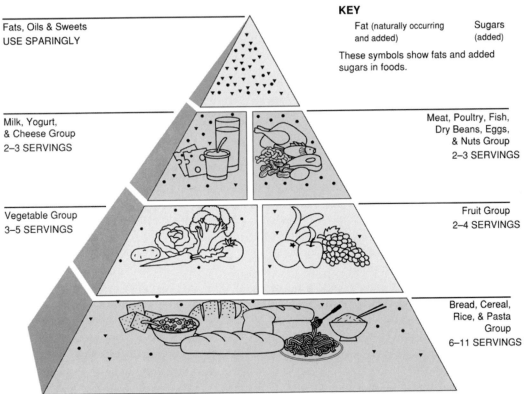

KEY

Fat (naturally occurring and added) ▼   Sugars (added) ●

These symbols show fats and added sugars in foods.

Fats, Oils & Sweets
USE SPARINGLY

Milk, Yogurt, & Cheese Group
2–3 SERVINGS

Meat, Poultry, Fish, Dry Beans, Eggs, & Nuts Group
2–3 SERVINGS

Vegetable Group
3–5 SERVINGS

Fruit Group
2–4 SERVINGS

Bread, Cereal, Rice, & Pasta Group
6–11 SERVINGS

SOURCE: U.S. Department of Agriculture/U.S. Department of Health and Human Services.

What counts as one serving?

Bread, Cereal, Rice & Pasta Group	Vegetable Group	Fruit Group	Milk, Cheese Group	Meat, Poultry, Fish Group
1 slice of bread	1 cup raw leafy veg.	1 medium fruit (apple, orange, banana)	1 cup nonfat milk	3 oz cooked lean meat+
1/2 cup of rice	1/2 baked white potato	3/4 cup juice	1 cup nonfat yogurt	3 oz sliced turkey+
1/2 cup of pasta	1/2 baked sweet potato	1/2 cup canned fruit	1.5 oz natural cheese*+	3 oz chicken breast+
1 oz of dry cereal	1/2 cup steamed veg.	1/2 cup grapes	1.5 oz processed cheese*+	1.5 cups kidney beans
1/2 cup oatmeal	1 cup lettuce	1/2 cup melon chunks	1/2 cup low-fat cottage cheese*+	3 eggs
1/2 bagel	1/2 cup carrot sticks			6 tbsp peanut butter
				1.5 cups lentils

* = foods that are high in fat
+ = foods that contain saturated fat or cholesterol

and at a BAC of 0.3%, a person could lapse into a coma. Death is likely with a BAC of 0.4% or higher.

These factors influence your BAC and response to alcohol:

- **How much and how quickly you drink.** If you chug your drinks, your liver which can only metabolize 0.5 oz of alcohol per hour, will not be able to keep up, resulting in a rapidly rising BAC.
- **The type of drink.** The stronger the drink, the faster the rise in BAC, and the consequent symptoms. If the drink contains water, juice, or milk, the rate of absorption will be decreased, slowing the rate of BAC rise. However, if you mix an alcoholic drink with carbon dioxide (e.g., champagne or a cola), the rate of alcohol absorption will increase.
- **The temperature of the alcoholic drink.** Warm drinks result in a faster rate of absorption.
- **Food.** Food slows the rate of absorption by interfering with the intestine's absorptive membrane surface. Certain high-fat foods can also prolong the time it takes for the stomach to empty its contents, resulting in delayed absorption times.
- **Your size.** Large people who have excessive fat or muscle tend to have a larger water volume, which dilutes the alcohol consumed. Therefore, large people can drink more alcohol and will get drunk more slowly than small or thin people.
- **Your sex.** Women tend to get drunk quicker than do men. Women possess smaller quantities of a stomach enzyme that metabolizes alcohol. The hormone estrogen also plays a role, as women are more sensitive to the effects of alcohol just prior to menstruation and when they are taking birth control pills that contain estrogen. One drink consumed by a woman will produce roughly the same physiologic consequences as two drinks consumed by a man.
- **Your age.** The older you are, the higher the BAC level will be after consuming equivalent drinks.
- **Your ethnicity.** Certain ethnic groups, such as Asians and Native Americans, are unable to metabolize alcohol as quickly as can Caucasians and African Americans. This results in higher BAC levels, as well as severe flushing and nausea.
- **Other drugs.** Mixing alcohol with certain common medications, such as aspirin, acetaminophen (Tylenol), and ulcer medications can cause the BAC to rise more rapidly. Some of the medications used to treat allergies and/or cold and flu symptoms may contain antihistamines that have side effects of drowsiness that are additive to the sedative effects of alcohol.

Prolonged alcohol consumption can lead to physical tolerance, as your brain becomes accustomed to a certain level of alcohol. You need to consume more alcohol to achieve the desired effects. This could lead to abuse and alcoholism.

Alcoholism is a chronic disease with genetic, physiologic, and psychosocial consequences. Like other addictions, alcoholism is characterized by the following: drinking more alcohol than intended; persistent desire but unsuccessful attempts to stop drinking; frequent withdrawal and absenteeism; decreased performance at school or work; continued drinking despite the realization that his/her drinking is causing physical, social, or psychological problems; the presence of withdrawal symptoms when not drinking; and the need for increasing amounts of alcohol to achieve intoxication.

Abusing Alcohol • • • • • • • • • • • • • •

The abuse of alcohol is no longer the cultural norm, even in many segments of the college student population. Responsible drinking is always up to you. What is the minimum legal age to drink? You do not need to drink to have a good time with friends. However, if you choose to drink alcohol, it is imperative that you also eat, to slow the rate of alcohol absorption into your body. Set a limit in advance on how many drinks you are going to have and stick to it. Always go to a party with a designated driver, a friend who in advance commits to not drinking. Also, do everything possible to prevent an intoxicated friend from driving.

Never use alcohol or other drugs as a means to relax; find alternative measures such as exercise, listening to music, reading, meditation, yoga, guided imagery, biofeedback, and hobbies to help you unwind.

Finally, don't drink alcohol just because you observe others drinking or because you believe "everyone else is doing it." According to national surveys, more students believe that others are using alcohol (95%) than what is actually the reality (85%). Students who choose not to drink excessively report "second-hand" effects of the irresponsible use of alcohol by their friends. These students are more likely to be physically assaulted or become a victim of sexual harassment on campus. Students' academic performance may also suffer due to impaired sleep (often to care for a roommate who had too much to drink), decreased study time, and poor concentration. As a result of these "second-hand" effects, more students are using alcohol responsibly as this is becoming the accepted campus norm.

Using Campus Resources •••••••

The Health Center on most campuses sponsors student organizations that provide information and consultations concerning alcohol and drug abuse prevention. BACCHUS (Boost Alcohol Consciousness Concerning the Health of University Students) is a national student organization that provides programs on responsible alcohol use, including National Collegiate Alcohol Awareness Week and the Safe Spring Break campaign. To find out more information, contact your campus Student Health Center or Counseling Center. They may have physicians or mental health professionals that can assist you or refer you to a community organization for treatment.

HIV Infection and AIDS •••••••••

We are experiencing an epidemic in the United States, actually a worldwide pandemic. Infection with the Human Immunodeficiency Virus (HIV) has become one of the most challenging infectious public health problems today, with far-reaching medical and psychosocial consequences. It is estimated that over 30 million people worldwide are infected with HIV with approximately 16,000 new infections occurring daily. In the United States, it is estimated that over one million people are living with HIV infection, with about one-third having Acquired Immunodeficiency Syndrome (AIDS), the terminal phase of the continuum of HIV infection. States with the highest incidence of HIV and AIDS are California, New York, Florida, and New Jersey. The incidence of HIV infection is highest in individuals between the ages of 20 and 29 years, with the incidence of AIDS highest during the fourth decade of life (i.e., between 30 and 39 years of age). In the United States, AIDS is now the second leading cause of death among people aged 25 to 44, and in many parts of the country, AIDS is now the number one cause of death among men in this same age range. Although the rate of infection is highest in men, the incidence of infection is steadily rising in women. The incidence of HIV infection is disproportionately higher among African Americans and Hispanics, when compared to Caucasians.

Epidemiology •••••••••••••••

The Human Immunodeficiency Virus (HIV) is very difficult to acquire. It is not spread through respiratory droplets or through casual contact, like the common cold or influenza viruses. You cannot acquire HIV by touching, simple kissing, hugging, or sitting next to someone who has the infection. HIV is not transmitted by sharing eating utensils, handshakes, using toilet seats, donating blood, or by mosquitoes.

There are only a few modes of HIV transmission. The virus is present in significant amounts only in blood, semen, vaginal secretions, and breast milk. The virus is present in very minute concentrations in saliva, such that there is essentially no risk of transmission via deep kissing. Transmission of HIV can occur as a result of:

- **Sexual activity.** HIV can be spread in semen and vaginal fluids during unprotected anal, vaginal, and oral sexual contact with an infected partner. Transmission is more likely to occur during anal intercourse than vaginal intercourse, and more likely to occur during vaginal intercourse compared to oral sex. Women are more likely to acquire HIV from an infected male partner than are men acquiring HIV infection from a female partner. The largest number of cases (50%) of HIV transmission have involved sexual contact between two men; however, the incidence of heterosexual transmission has been rising at an alarming pace over the past seven years, and is currently over 20 percent.
- **Injections using shared needles.** Any contaminated needle can transmit the virus, making steroid use, tattoos, and body piercing potentially risky unless sterile needles are used.
- **Perinatally.** A baby may acquire the virus before birth (via the mother's circulation through the placenta), during the birth process (via vaginal secretions), or after birth (via infected breast milk). Mothers who are HIV positive have a 25 percent chance of infecting their unborn baby; this number decreases to less than 7 percent if the mother receives treatment during pregnancy.
- **Transfusions of blood, blood products, or organ transplants from HIV-infected individuals.** Since March 1985, the blood supply has been tested for the presence of HIV, significantly decreasing the incidence of HIV transmission via this means. Changes in the methods of screening blood donors have also helped with this decline. However, the risk still is present albeit very small.

Figure 8.4 Guidelines for Condom Use

- Always use a latex condom rather than a natural membrane condom.
- Store condoms in a cool, dry place; never store them in the car or in your wallet.
- Do not use condoms beyond their expiration date.
- Only use water-based lubricants, such as K-Y Jelly; oil-based lubricants will break down the latex.
- Use spermicide containing nonoxynol-9, as this compound inactivates HIV.
- Know how to use a condom properly; practice if necessary.
- Do not reuse a condom.
- ALWAYS use one!

Testing for HIV

The most widely used tests to determine the presence of HIV infection actually do not detect the virus itself, but measure the presence of antibodies that the body forms in response to infection with HIV. The standard laboratory blood tests that are most commonly used are the Enzyme Linked Immunoassay (ELISA) and the Western Blot. The Ora-Sure is a type of ELISA test that detects the presence of HIV antibody in the mouth mucosa rather than in the blood; the accuracy of the Ora-Sure test is about the same as for the blood test. The Western Blot is a more specific and expensive test and is therefore primarily used as a confirmatory test when the ELISA comes back as positive. The Western Blot is performed on the same blood specimen which resulted in the positive ELISA. If the ELISA is positive and the Western Blot is negative, the person does not have HIV infection. If the ELISA and the confirmatory Western Blot tests are both positive, then the person is diagnosed as having the HIV infection. Since it takes at least two weeks to six months for the body to produce enough HIV antibodies to be measured by the tests, a negative result obtained on a test done too soon after the last risky behavior may not be accurate. Therefore, it is imperative that the ELISA be performed at least one additional time, preferably about six months later. Approximately 95 percent of people who have been infected with HIV will have ELISA blood tests reveal a positive result within the first six months.

Anyone who feels they may be at risk should be tested for HIV. Early testing is important because treatments with various types of nucleoside inhibitors and the powerful protease inhibitors suppress proliferation of HIV and in most cases lower the numbers of viruses in the bloodstream to undetectable levels, leading to a delay in the onset of AIDS symptoms. The use of protease inhibitors in combination with nucleoside inhibitors as a therapeutic "drug cocktail", however, does *not* represent a cure. To date, there is no cure for HIV and education remains the key ingredient in prevention.

Limit Your Risk

NO ONE IS IMMUNE! Your risk of acquiring HIV infection is not dependent on who you are, but is dependent on your behaviors. The only absolutely safe way to protect yourself is by abstaining from sexual activity. However, if you do choose to have sexual intercourse, you should ALWAYS use a condom, even if you think that your partner is not infected. You can never be certain of your partner's past sexual history or drug use history, because he/she may have acquired HIV from a previous partner several years ago. Unknown to both of you, your partner may have slept with someone who slept with someone who once secretly abused injection drugs. Remember, once an individual becomes infected with HIV, they can remain completely asymptomatic for many years. They may not even know that they have the infection! Therefore, next to abstinence, the safest way to protect yourself is to always use a latex condom.

How confident do you feel that you will practice safer sex? Take Exercise 8.2 to find out.

Interactive Web Sites

There are a number of interactive web sites you can visit to learn more about health and wellness issues. The ones listed below contain information that may be of particular interest to college students and young adults. They are listed by topic for your convenience. Visit some of these sites as your time and interests dictate.

Health Assessments

- **LiveWell Health Risk Appraisal**
  http://wellness.uwsp.edu/Health_Service/services/livewell
  This comprehensive site sponsored by the National Wellness Institute features a series of self-assessment surveys composed of questions in a variety of wellness dimensions, including physical fitness, nutrition, self-care, drugs, emotional health, spiritual wellness, and others.
- **Selfgrowth.com**
  http://www.selfgrowth.com
  This site is an online guide to self-help, self-improvement, and personal growth, featuring information on psychology, dieting, recovery, relationships, health and fitness, natural medicine, spiritual development, newsletter, an online IQ test, and general topics and organization.

Physical Fitness

- **Shape Up America!**
  http://www.shapeup.org
  This web site provides information about safe weight management, healthy eating, and physical fitness, including an online library, body fat lab, support center, the "Shape Up and Drop 10" feature for personalized fitness and diet recommendations, and more.

Stress

- **Stress Assess**
  http://wellness.uwsp.edu/Health_Service/services/stress.html
  This site features a comprehensive educational tool to help assess your current stress sources, distress symptoms and lifestyle behaviors. It is not a clinical or diagnostic tool. Based on your personalized assessment, you can learn healthy and effective strategies to balance the stress in your life.

Mental Health

- **Wellplace**
  http://www.wellplace.com
  This site is sponsored by Pioneer Behavioral Health and features fact sheets on a variety of mental health topics, including depression, stress, PTSD, and personality disorders. In addition, the site has several self assessment tools, wellness articles, chat forums, ask the experts, and a list of online resources for self-help recovery groups and national hotlines.
- **National Mental Health Information Center**
  http://www.mentalhealth.org
  This site, sponsored by the National Mental Health Information Center of the U.S. Department of Health and Human Services, features current mental health topics, including PTSD, children's mental health, substance abuse prevention, suicide prevention, and a comprehensive list of online mental health resources.

Nutrition

- **Nutrition.gov**
  http://www.nutrition.gov
  This is an excellent online source for comprehensive nutrition information, including dietary guidelines, food pyramid, food labels, education programs, dietary supplements, healthy diets, health management, food safety, a description on how the body uses nutrients found in food, biotechnology, research, and current nutrition news.
- **CyberDiet Tools**
  http://www.CyberDiet.com/tools/assess.html
  Dedicated to the belief that healthy weight management and lifestyle change must come from a combination of balanced nutrition, regular exercise and behavioral modification, CyberDiet provides a wealth of fun and well-presented nutritional information. Cyberdiet.com provides a comprehensive resource for those seeking a change to a healthier lifestyle by providing interactive tools to calculate body mass index, body fat distribution, and target heart rate.
- **Count Your Calories Because Your Calories Count:**
  http://www.bgsm.edu/nutrition/in.html
  This interactive site sponsored by Wake Forest University Baptist Medical Center features a four-step assessment of your diet, including "How's Your Diet" a personalized diet assessment linked to the Food Guide Pyramid recommendations, "Fit or Not Quiz", "The Calorie Counter", and "Drive Though Diet" where you can assess the nutrition of popular foods from several fast food restaurants. There is also an "Eating Disorders" quiz.

- **Something's Fishy Website on Eating Disorders**
  http://www.something-fishy.org
  This comprehensive web site features a wealth of information on all types of eating disorders, as well as current news, how to help, signs and symptoms, cultural issues, doctors and patients, prevention, online support, as well as an online newsletter.

Alcohol, Smoking, and Drug Abuse

- **Partnership for a Drug-free America**
  http://www.drugfreeamerica.org
  This is a very comprehensive site featuring current resources and photographs on a variety of drugs, including a special site on ecstasy and club drugs. This site also features resources and several video clips and true life stories revealing the consequences of drug use.
- **Truth—Smoking Awareness and Prevention**
  http://www.wholetruth.com
  This interactive site provides answers to common myths and questions pertaining to cigarette smoking in an entertaining way, targeted at teens and young adults.
- **Facts On Tap: Alcohol and Your College Experience.**
  http://www.factsontap.org
  This colorful and interactive web site is designed specifically for college students and features a variety of activities and straightforward information specifically written for college students. Some of the topics include: alcohol and the college experience, the effects of alcohol on the non-drinker, alcohol and the family, and a true/false quiz to test your knowledge about alcohol and its effects.

Safer Sex, HIV/AIDS and other STD's

- **Sexually Transmitted Disease Risk Profiler.**
  http://www.unspeakable.com/profiler/profiler.html
  This site designed specifically for college students has two interactive sections. First, the Risk Profiler can help you determine where your risk of acquiring an STD lies. It takes your answers to thirteen questions about your age, gender, sexual history, and behavior, and shows you how these factors play a part in creating your own personal risk profile. The second interactive site is a ten-question STD Quiz that will give you an opportunity to test your knowledge of STDs, and learn more about their symptoms, prevention, and treatment.
- **Sexuality information from Columbia University "Go Ask Alice"**
  http://www.goaskalice.columbia.edu/Cat6.html
  This site, created by the Columbia University Health Education program features a variety of questions and answers to questions pertaining to relationships, sexuality, and sexual health.

Summary

In this chapter, we discussed several important ways to enable you to live a balanced, healthy life. Health is something to be cherished. A healthy student is one that will excel academically, be more productive, and have time to pursue recreational pursuits and spend quality time with family and friends. A healthier student is a happier and more productive student with greater self-esteem and better coping skills. A healthy person is also a happier son or daughter, a better friend, a more productive employee, and a more respected contributor to society. Healthy decision-making while in college will pay big physical and psychosocial dividends, with benefits that will last for many years after you graduate. Here's to your health!

Name _____ Date_____

Exercise 8.1 Wellness Lifestyle Assessment

DIRECTIONS: Using the following scale, answer each statement by placing the number that most closely corresponds to your lifestyle and feelings in the space preceding each statement.

KEY:
1 = "no/never" or "don't know"
2 = "rarely" or "1–6 times a year"
3 = "occasionally" or "1–4 times a month"
4 = "often, frequently" or "2–5 times a week"
5 = "yes/always" or "almost daily"

A. Physical Assessment

_____ 1. I perform aerobic exercises for twenty minutes or more per session.

_____ 2. When participating in physical activities, I include stretching and flexibility exercises.

_____ 3. My body fat composition is appropriate for my gender. (Men: 10-18%; Women: 16-25%)

_____ 4. I have appropriate medical checkups regularly and keep records of test results.

_____ 5. I practice safer sex or abstinence. I never have sex when intoxicated.

B. Nutritional Assessment

_____ 1. I eat at least 3 to 5 servings of vegetables and 2 to 4 servings of fruits daily.

_____ 2. I eat at least 6 to 11 servings daily of foods from the bread, cereal, rice, and pasta group.

_____ 3. I choose or prepare foods that tend to be lower in cholesterol and saturated fat.

_____ 4. When purchasing foods, I read the "Nutrition Facts" labels.

_____ 5. I avoid adding salt to my food.

C. Alcohol and Drugs Assessment

_____ 1. I avoid smoking and using smokeless tobacco products.

_____ 2. I avoid drinking alcohol or limit my daily alcohol intake to two drinks or less.

_____ 3. I do not drive after drinking alcohol or after taking medications that make me sleepy.

_____ 4. I follow directions when taking both prescription and over-the-counter medications.

_____ 5. I keep a record of drugs to which I am allergic in my wallet or purse.

D. Emotional Wellness Assessment

_____ 1. I feel positive about myself and my life. I set realistic goals for myself.

_____ 2. I can effectively cope with life's ups and downs in a healthy manner.

_____ 3. I do not tend to be nervous, impatient, or under a high amount of stress.

_____ 4. I can express my feelings of anger.

_____ 5. When working under pressure, I stay calm and am not easily distracted.

E. Intellectual Wellness Assessment

_____ 1. I seek advice when I am uncertain or uncomfortable with a recommended treatment.

_____ 2. I ask about the risks, benefits, and medical necessity of all medical tests and procedures.

_____ 3. I keep informed of the latest trends and information concerning health matters.

_____ 4. I feel comfortable about talking to my doctor.

_____ 5. I know the guidelines for practicing good preventive medicine and self-care.

F. Social and Spiritual Wellness Assessment

_____ 1. I am able to develop close, intimate relationships.

_____ 2. I am involved in school and/or community activities.

_____ 3. I have recreational hobbies and do something fun just for myself at least once a week.

_____ 4. I know what my values and beliefs are and I am tolerant of the beliefs of others.

_____ 5. My life has meaning and direction. I have life goals. Personal reflection is important.

ANALYZING YOUR WELLNESS ASSESSMENT

For each of the six wellness sections, add the total number of points that you assigned to each question. Place the totals of each section below:

TOTALS for each of the six sections:

A. Physical Assessment. . . . .   _____

B. Nutritional Assessment . . . .   _____

C. Alcohol and Drugs Assessment . . . .   _____

D. Emotional Wellness Assessment. . . . .   _____

E. Intellectual Wellness Assessment . . . .   _____

F. Social and Spiritual Wellness Assessment. . . . .   _____

TOTAL POINTS. . . . .   _____

Then, divide the Total Points by 6 to get the "Average Wellness Score" =   _____

What do your results mean? The results apply to each of the six individual sections, as well as for determining your overall wellness assessment (after dividing your total score by six).

Total for each section (or Average Wellness Score)	RESULTS (for each individual section and for the overall assessment)
23–25	Excellent Your lifestyle choices and attitudes can significantly contribute to a healthy life. You are commended!
19–22	Good You engage in many health-promoting behaviors and attitudes. You care about your health. However, there are some areas that you could improve to provide optimal health benefits and wellness.
11–18	Average You are typical of the average American who tends to not always practice the healthiest of behaviors, despite having the knowledge which would suggest the contrary. Now is the time to consider making changes in your lifestyle to foster a healthier future.
5–10	Needs immediate improvement You are to be commended for being concerned enough about your health to take this assessment, but your behaviors and attitudes may be having a detrimental effect on your overall health. Now is the time to take action to improve your health!

⋯⋯⋯⋯ **Exercise 8.2 Can You Practice Safer Sex?** ⋯⋯⋯⋯

Most people know how HIV is transmitted and what behaviors are necessary to reduce their risk of acquiring the virus. However, some of these behaviors are not always easy to do. Your confidence in yourself to perform these protective sex behaviors is as important as simply knowing what the behaviors are. Assess your safer sex confidence level by answering these questions honestly, according to the key below:

KEY:

A = I always could do this in all situations.
B = I could do this occasionally.
C = I could not do this.

_____ 1. buy condoms at a store.

_____ 2. discuss using a condom with a new sex partner before having sex.

_____ 3. refuse to have sex with a person if he/she did not want to use a condom.

_____ 4. talk to a new sex partner about his/her past sexual experiences and number of sexual partners.

_____ 5. ask a new sex partner whether he/she has ever had sex with another person of the same sex.

_____ 6. ask a potential sex partner about the use of intravenous drugs and sharing of needles.

_____ 7. be able to avoid using alcohol on a date to help make a decision about sex easier.

_____ 8. be able to clearly express what my sexual expectations and limits are before beginning any sexual activity.

_____ 9. be able to resist an unwanted sexual advance or stop sexual activity if a condom wasn't available.

_____ 10. be able to resist an unwanted sexual activity even when slightly intoxicated after a few drinks.

What do my results mean?

1) Multiply the number of responses you answered with "C" by 2.
2) Add to the result, the number of responses you answered with "B."
3) Responses answered with "A" do not count as points.
4) Add the answers from 1) + 2) above to get the "Confidence Score."
5) Circle your overall confidence score on the continuum below to determine your risk.

| 0 | 2 | 4 | 6 | 8 | 10 | 12 | 14 | 16 | 18 | 20 |

LOW RISK   HIGH RISK

If you scored between 10 and 20 points, you tend to doubt your ability to behave in a way that would protect you from acquiring HIV. You should evaluate your own beliefs and attitudes concerning safer sex in the four areas assessed: condom use, self-protection, sex under the influence, and sexual limits.

Planning for a Career

"Destiny is not a matter of chance, but a matter of choice. It is not a thing to be waited for, it is a thing to be achieved."
—William Jennings Bryan

Making Career Decisions • • • • • • • •

Making career decisions is a lifelong task. You have already begun the process by deciding to go to college. The courses you take, your choice of major, the work experience you accumulate, the clubs and groups you join, and the people you meet may influence the career decisions you make in your lifetime.

Chances are you are already thinking about your choice of major and related career options. Don't be alarmed if you feel uncertain or have no ideas about your career plans. Now is the time to question, explore, and wonder. It can be reassuring to know that many sources of career information and systems of career decision making already exist to help you in this task.

Before we get into a discussion of what goes into career decision making, let's explore some popular myths that might sabotage your efforts to make informed decisions.

Career Myths • • • • • • • • • • • • • • • •

1. "I don't need to think about my career now; I'm just starting college."
   Graduation may be years away—but the process of career planning has already begun. Knowing who you are and what you are looking for will better enable you to find satisfying career options. And self-assessment takes time!
2. "I want to take **THAT TEST** that will tell me what I should be."
   There is **NO** test that will tell you what you should be or what career you should follow. Different types of career assessments can be useful in gathering information about you and relating it to career clusters. Test results often help you to put information in order so you can verify or challenge your ideas. These assessments are tools; the decision is yours.
3. "I'll pursue whatever career is in demand."
   Knowing what's "hot" in the job market is important information, but not the only information you need to make a decision. Without knowing about your own interests and skills, you may choose a career that's available, but later you may find you are not suited for it.
4. "I need to find the perfect career."
   There is no "perfect" career. What you will discover is that there are several ways you can find a meaningful career. No one gets 100 percent of

what he/she wants. There is usually compromise. Your task is to identify what you want and need from your career, put these features into priority, and use this information as a guide in making your career decisions.

5. "If I make the wrong decision, I'll be stuck forever."
   Fear of making the wrong decision can prevent you from making any decision. When making career decisions you'll find that nothing is written in stone. Few people head into one career and stay there for their whole working lives. The U.S. Bureau of Labor Statistics estimates that the average worker will change careers five times during a work life.
6. "Everyone knows what major/career they want but me."
   It may seem like everyone is decided but you. However, statistics show that most students change majors (and career plans) several times while in college. It is better to recognize that you are undecided and go about finding the necessary information to make your decisions, than to assume you have it all figured out and never evaluate your plan.

Career/Life Planning Process • • • • •

So, how do you get started with career planning? Let's begin with a definition of the Career/Life Planning Process, which involves three components:

Career/Life—Your career decisions will include more than which job to take upon graduation. Your career is the sum of all the work experiences you will have. The work you choose to pursue will have a direct impact on the way you live your life. Your career decisions cannot be made in a vacuum, but should be made within the context of your lifestyle preferences.

Planning—Webster defines planning as "formulating a program to accomplish or attain something." It is purposeful and done ahead of time. Therefore, career/life planning implies setting short- and long-range goals about your work and lifestyle with specific objectives that will help you meet them.

Process—Your career plan will not be the result of one decision you make, but rather a series of decisions throughout your lifetime. You will go through

This chapter was written by Dr. Beverly Dalrymple, Director of the Center for Leadership Development and Civic Responsibility at Florida International University. It is used by permission of the author.

the steps in career planning several times because as you continue to grow and develop as a person, your interests, skills, and values will also change. The job market definitely changes, sometimes beyond your control. So "process" implies a dynamic aspect of developing satisfying and successful career and life plans.

The whole process might seem overwhelming, but the career/life planning process can be broken down into three basic steps with specific tasks to accomplish. Figure 9.1 The Process of Career/Life Planning is a picture of this process.

Step One—Understanding Yourself Requires Self-Assessment

Knowing about yourself is the basis of career decision making. This includes identifying your interests—what you like and dislike; your skills—what you do well; your values—what is important to you about your work; and your personality traits or characteristics—how you behave as a person.

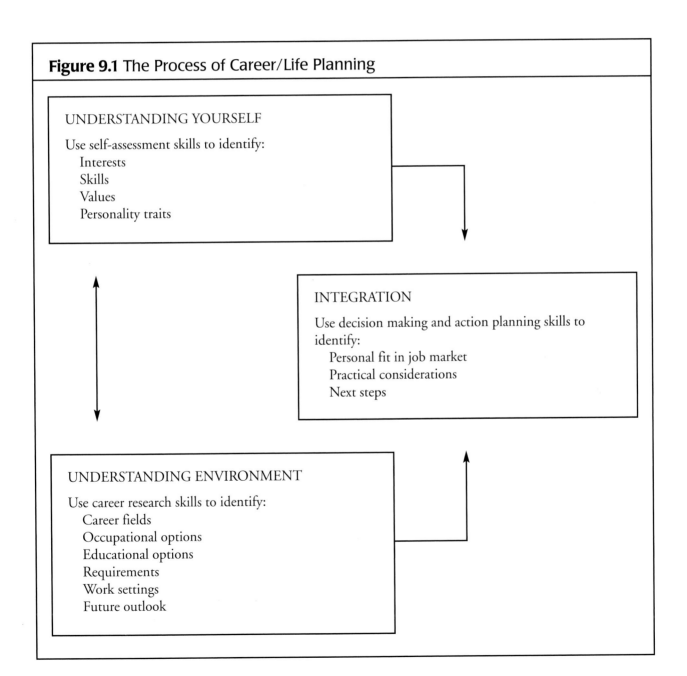

Figure 9.1 The Process of Career/Life Planning

UNDERSTANDING YOURSELF

Use self-assessment skills to identify:
    Interests
    Skills
    Values
    Personality traits

INTEGRATION

Use decision making and action planning skills to identify:
    Personal fit in job market
    Practical considerations
    Next steps

UNDERSTANDING ENVIRONMENT

Use career research skills to identify:
    Career fields
    Occupational options
    Educational options
    Requirements
    Work settings
    Future outlook

Interests

Begin the self-assessment process by taking a good look at your own interests. This self-assessment step includes analyzing activities that you like and dislike to identify patterns in your interests. Your interest patterns can give clues about the type of work or work environment you might enjoy or want to avoid. Complete Exercise 9.1 to start identifying activities that interest you. Activities that you engage in for pleasure or leisure can tell you a lot about similar work functions that you might find motivating and interesting in a career.

Skills

Sound career decision making requires a realistic critique of your skills. What are you good at doing? What functions are harder for you or require more development? What have you noticed about your academic skills so far? Identifying your skills and abilities can help you make realistic decisions about programs of study and future work. Aptitude testing is one way to analyze your skills. It requires going to a certified test administrator and it is usually time consuming and expensive. These services may be available on your campus or in your community.

A practical way to assess your skills is to analyze your experiences. A good method for analyzing what you have already done is to consider your accomplishments. These experiences do not have to be grand, such as finding a cure for cancer or the answer to world peace, or fit anyone else's definition of accomplishment. The accomplishments should be some things you feel good about from your life (college, work, leisure, and relationships). These are usually experiences that presented a challenge and satisfaction in achieving, such as:

• passed chemistry
• ran a 10K race
• volunteered in a nursing home
• researched family tree
• elected student body president

After you identify your accomplishments, write a short description of what you did to accomplish each task. Identify the skills you used in each accomplishment by highlighting how you worked with people, data, things, or ideas as you completed each task.

Summarize your reflections. Notice the patterns in the skills you used in each accomplishment. You might begin your career exploration by researching careers that require these types of skills. Complete Exercise 9.2 to review your accomplishments.

Values

Values identify what is important to you. Work values describe what is important about the work you do. It is useful to identify values when considering possible careers because they may tell you about work related needs, motivators, and long-term satisfaction. Complete Exercise 9.3 for help in clarifying your work related values.

Personality Traits

Career decision making requires tackling some tough questions, such as "Who am I?" "What motivates me?" and "What's my style for doing things?" These are not easy questions to answer. Becoming self-observant and developing reflection skills can help you to address this aspect of self-assessment. Your personality traits can reveal a lot about what motivates you in work and help you to assess a career with the best "fit" for you. Try Exercise 9.4 to begin this aspect of your self-assessment. Share your insights with someone who knows you and compare notes.

Summarize

Pull together the information from your self-assessment activities by completing Exercise 9.5 Your Personal Career Profile. Do you notice a pattern or relationship among your interests, skills, values, and personality traits? What implications might these similarities have on careers that could be interesting to you? Incorporate what you have learned about yourself into a statement about your "ideal job." Use your ideal job as a guideline for exploring the many career opportunities that will allow you to satisfy your unique combination of interests, skills, values, and personality traits.

Continue to evaluate all of your experiences—work, school, and hobbies—on a regular basis. This process can turn up characteristics you might find satisfying in your future career. And remember, identifying what you don't want can be as helpful as finding what you do want. Both help define what you are looking for.

Step Two—Understanding the Environment Requires Conducting Career Research

The U.S. Bureau of Labor classifies over 20,000 different occupations. These occupations are often grouped into career clusters that share similar job functions, skills, or training requirements. It's impossible to know every job that's in the workforce, but you should be familiar with the general categories such as:

Agriculture/Home Economics
Arts/Humanities
Business
Education/Welfare
Engineering/Architecture
Government/Law
Health
Industry/Trade
Services
Science
Technology

The following list of career references can help you explore specific occupations in each cluster. You can find these reference books in the university library, the career services office, or any public library. All of the publications by the U.S. Department of Labor are also available on their website (www.bls.gov).

Dictionary of Occupational Titles, published by the U.S. Department of Labor, gives standardized and comprehensive descriptions of job duties and related information for 20,000 occupations. Each job title has a nine-digit code number.

Occupational Outlook Handbook, published by the U.S. Department of Labor, describes what workers do on the job, working conditions, the training and education needed, earnings, expected job prospects.

Occupational Outlook quarterly, published by the U.S. Department of Labor. This magazine offers articles featuring various occupations. The **Quarterly** often features unusual, interesting, overlooked possibilities. One issue per year reviews job prospects for all major occupations.

Guide for Occupational Exploration, published by JIST for the U.S. Department of Labor, describes 2,500 job titles by interest, skills required, and industry. It is cross-referenced to other career books.

Encyclopedia of Careers, published in four volumes by J.G. Ferguson Publishing Co., describes careers by general categories such as: professional, technical, special fields. Also included are industry profiles.

Internet Sources. There are many electronic sources for career-related information. Since actual website addresses can change frequently, try starting with a keyword search using the word "career" or enter the career you are interested in, followed by "employment".

As you conduct your research, be sure to locate the following information:

Job description
Skills required
Education or training requirements
Work environment
Salary projections
Future outlook
Related occupations

Step Three—Integration Requires Decision-Making and Action Planning

This is probably the most important step because integration requires taking what you know about yourself and putting it together with the reality of the work world. In doing so, you begin to identify and evaluate career options that are practical for you. Questions to consider:

What career clusters am I interested in?
What career fields are found in these clusters?
What specific occupations are found in these career fields?
What type of preparation is needed for these jobs?
Does the university offer these programs of study?
Do I have the academic strengths to pursue that major?
What challenges might be presented in the job market (competition, relocation)?
Do I have the time, money, and support resources to pursue these options?
What else do I need to know in order to identify my career objective?

Choosing a Major ••••••••••••

Choosing a major is part of the career planning process. The same type of self-assessment, information gathering, and decision-making skills described in this chapter can be used in exploring and selecting an appropriate program of study. Your choice of major should be compatible with your interests, academic skills, and career goals. You can approach the task from two different directions—from careers that interest you or subjects you enjoy learning. Some helpful tips are listed below.

Career Interest Approach ••••••••

Identify careers that interest you by using the career planning process described in Figure 9.1.

Research the educational requirements necessary for each career.

Use the college catalog to explore the academic programs available to you.

Assess your ability to be successful in the required courses.

Talk to other students in the major and to an academic advisor about the specific aspects of the program of study.

Take a class in the area to test your interest, ideas, and skills.

Favorite Subject Approach ••••••••

Identify the subjects that interest you.

Research the careers that are related to these subjects. A good online resource can be found at *www.fiu.edu/~careers/student/explore_under_what canidowithmymajor.htm.*

Explore work functions, entry-level requirements, and job market trends.

Use your college catalog to explore the academic programs available to you.

Talk to other students in the major and to an academic advisor about the specific aspects of the program of study.

Take a class in the area to test your ideas, interest, and skills.

Remember that some careers have specific educational requirements for entry into the profession, such as physical therapy or engineering. Other careers are not limited to a specific undergraduate major. Employers look for candidates that can think critically, communicate effectively, and continue to learn on the job. Your track record as a student can demonstrate to employers that you have what it takes to be a productive employee.

Gathering and evaluating information is a critical part of choosing a major and making career plans. Here are some additional information resources.

Career Services

Most campus Career Services offices provide career advising, career reference materials, employer literature, and job search information. Computerized career guidance programs, such as SIGI Plus, DISCOVER, or CHOICES, are excellent tools for self-assessment and career exploration. Services might also be available for student employment, internships, resume writing, interview preparation, and Internet searches.

Informational Interviewing

Another way to get information is to talk to people about their jobs. This can be on a casual basis, such as talking with family and friends, or it can be done in a formal way by contacting experienced professionals in your field of interest and scheduling an appointment to meet with them. Either way, you are interviewing for information. This technique is an excellent way to get inside information that might not be available in written sources. It also helps you to develop your communication skills and a professional network that you will need in your future career. Try Exercise 9.6, Informational Interviewing, to gather career information and practice your interviewing skills.

Experience

After you have gathered substantial information, the next thing to do is test your ideas through some first-hand experience. Many people find they learn best by doing; this is described as experiential learning. Experiential learning programs include cooperative education, internships, and career-related volunteer work. Work experience helps you get a first-hand look at your intended career field. This real

---

Figure 9.2 Your College Guide for Career Success

Educational and Career Tasks

FRESHMAN

Explore Career Areas
Visit campus career center
    for orientation on programs & services
Talk with parents, friends, professors, and
    counselor about your career ideas
Complete career assessments
Identify the following:
    interests
    abilities
    career-related hobbies
    personality style
    career values

SOPHOMORE

Collect Information
Research careers in the library
Conduct info interview
List 5 career options for your intended
    majors
Select electives to test career ideas
Confirm major
Explore experiential options to test career skills and
    ideas

JUNIOR

Increase Experience
Apply for Intern/Co-op assignment
Develop your resume
Attend Law/Grad School Info Fair
Take leadership role in student club/group
Attend Career Fairs

SENIOR

Implement Career Plan
Register with Career Services office
Attend training session on:
    Resume/Cover Letter Writing
    Interviewing Skills
    Resume Critique
Develop list of targeted employers
Send out graduate school applications
Network, network, network

world opportunity will allow you to develop experience for your resume, meet employers, apply what you are learning in the classroom, and evaluate the fit of this career. Participation in experiential learning programs is usually competitive and requires planning. Make it part of your college agenda. Contact the Career Services office at your college for more information.

Another excellent way to develop experience that will be helpful to you in your career planning is to become involved on campus. Most colleges offer a variety of student clubs and organizations, and many of them are focused on a career field or program of study. Become an *active* member—help plan an event, start a new tradition, or provide a service. Consider taking a leadership role in an organization or with student government. You will learn valuable information about yourself, such as your ability to work with others, to make decisions, to solve problems, and to communicate. The skills you develop through campus involvement—teamwork, planning, and leadership—are similar to the organizational skills employers seek in the workplace. Contact the student activities or campus life office on your campus to see how you can get involved.

Summary

As you can see, there are many career planning tasks you can be working on during your first year. Remember the three steps in the process: Self-Assessment, Career Research, and Decision Making/Action Planning. "Your College Guide to Career Success" will serve as a handy guide and reminder of career-related things to do during your college program. It also provides suggestions for making and implementing your career plans for the future. Start using it today!

Name _____   Date_____

By answering the questions below you will start to highlight activities you enjoy.

1. What subjects do you like?

2. What books or magazines do you read?

3. What do you like to do for fun? What do you do in your spare time?

4. What jobs have you had? What did you like or dislike about them? (Remember to include volunteer work.)

5. Based on your responses, write a short statement about the things you like to do, and why. What types of activities are included or excluded?

·················· **Exercise 9.2 Accomplishments** ··················

Identify five accomplishments. Write a short description of each, including the situation, your actions, and the outcome. What challenges did you face? How did you overcome them?

1.

2.

3.

4.

5.

Now, select three of your accomplishments. List each one on a separate piece of paper. Complete this part of your self-assessment by answering the following questions regarding each accomplishment:

- What skills did you use?

- How did you interact with people?

- Did you work alone or with others?

- Did it require you to be a leader or team member?

- How did you deal with data, ideas, and/or things?

- Which did you enjoy the most?

- What was most difficult?

- What was most rewarding?

- How much structure was involved?

- What interests are represented? Art, music, sports, travel, animals, science, etc.?

- What values are represented? Helping society, competition, influencing people, fame, self-expression, excitement, etc.?

·········   # Exercise 9.3 Values Checklist   ··························

Following is a partial list of work values, with an example of each. Read the list and examples of each value when applied to work settings. Rate each value according to the scale below.

Rate each work value: V if it is very important; S if it is somewhat important; or N if it is not important.

Adventure	_____	take risks in work
Creativity	_____	developing new ideas or things
Authority	_____	being in charge
Altruism	_____	helping others
Independence	_____	plan own work schedule/work without close supervision
Travel	_____	opportunities to travel on the job
Prestige	_____	be recognized and respected for the work I do
Stability	_____	keep a routine without surprises
Variety	_____	experience change and enjoy different tasks
Family	_____	have time and energy to spend with family
Teamwork	_____	work as a member of a team
Learning	_____	opportunity to learn new skills and apply them on the job
Challenge	_____	use your skills and abilities to solve complex problems
Advancement	_____	opportunity for promotion
Leisure	_____	have time out of work to pursue other interests
Wealth	_____	have a high income

Of course, just identifying what you want is not realistic. There is no guarantee that you will be able to satisfy all of the values that are very important to you. Compromise will be a necessity. From your list of Very Important values, choose five that you believe are most important (probably things you will not be able to live without). Now prioritize these five values on the list below.

1.

2.

3.

4.

5.

Name _____ Date_____

List 10 words that describe you.

1.   6.

2.   7.

3.   8.

4.   9.

5.   10.

Which words identify work-related strengths or assets?

Which identify work-related weaknesses or liabilities?

·············· **Exercise 9.5 Personal Career Profile** ····················

Use this space to summarize your self-information.

List three interests you have identified:

1.

2.

3.

List three activities or things you wish to avoid:

1.

2.

3.

List three skills you feel are your strengths:

1.

2.

3.

List three work-related values:

1.

2.

3.

List three personality traits:

1.

2.

3.

Write a short statement describing your "ideal" job.

···· **Exercise 9.6 Organizing an Informational Interview** ····

First, start with relatives, friends, and co-workers or referrals from people you know. If you feel comfortable, identify people in positions of interest in your community and formally contact them for an Informational Interview. If you are contacting strangers, you might begin by introducing yourself as a college student doing research on. . . . (your career of interest). Most people are willing to talk about what they do; just be sure to respect their time and busy schedule. Therefore, always have your questions prepared in advance and arrive on time.

Next, develop questions for your Informational Interview. Feel free to add new questions to this sample list. Once you begin the interview, record the responses for processing later.

1. How did you decide upon this occupation?

2. What are your major responsibilities on the job?

3. What is your typical day like?

4. What do you like best about the work you do? What do you like least?

5. What are the latest trends in this field?

6. What training and skills are necessary for a career in this area?

7. What advice would you give to someone who is planning for a career in this field?

8. Can you recommend someone else whom I should talk to in this field?

Finally, write a short summary of your experience. What did you learn that might help you in planning for your career?

CHAPTER 10

Making the Most of College

*"Life's more persistent and urgent question is,
what are you doing for others?"*
—Martin Luther King, Jr.

Where to from Here? • • • • • • • • •

You've now made it through the semester! (See, it wasn't so bad after all, was it?!) What's next?

Hopefully, it was a successful semester for most of you. For some, unfortunately, there may have been too many of those roadblocks and other obstacles we warned you about. Adjustment to the college environment may have been more than you anticipated, but now that you have a semester under your belt, you are better prepared for next term if you use what you've learned.

In the past semester, you've learned about how to succeed in a university. We hope that this course helped prepare you for that success. Even if much of the information you were given in the course isn't applicable yet, you will find that many of the suggestions will help you avoid future hassles that otherwise could stall your progress.

A simple suggestion such as remembering to regularly check your records in the Registrar's Office and keeping all your academic information current and accurate could save you from trouble at a later point in your academic career. Just imagine waiting until your last semester to check your transcript, only to learn that you are one credit or one class short of the requirements for graduation!

You should now feel right at home at the university. The early fears and hesitations about college life should be far behind you. That doesn't mean that you are home free or that nothing will ever go wrong. You've still got a long way to go before graduation!

When you receive your semester's grades, you will have the first indicator of your potential for success as a college student. Depending on the courses you took, however, don't be misled into thinking that college is easier than you thought it was going to be! Some courses may be harder and will demand more time than others. As you advance toward a degree, study and class preparation time will need to increase.

Most students find that two hours of study for every hour spent in class is a good guide. That may seem extreme, but by the time you review your notes after each class, read the assignment for the next class, and complete homework, you will have spent the nearly six hours weekly for every three-credit class you take.

You should have learned how to better manage time and stress. Some students find it difficult to juggle work, academics, and a social life. Undoubtedly you had to make compromises, and in some cases, eliminate some activities just to manage the necessities.

Now that you are a full-fledged college student and have adjusted to an academic routine, you will face other important decisions. These decisions may include: moving into an apartment or into a campus residence hall; whether or not to pledge a fraternity or sorority or join one or several student organizations; and whether or not to change your academic major.

Remember to be cautious about individuals who ask you to join their organization. Ask questions about the group and check with the Activities Office on campus to ascertain that the organization is recognized and legitimate.

Get Involved! • • • • • • • • • • • • • • • • •

Getting involved on campus can be one of the most important decisions you can make. Many students go through their entire academic careers without getting involved in even one club or activity on campus. These students often are at a disadvantage when they start the job interviewing process or apply to graduate or professional schools. Take a look at an application for graduate or professional school. You will find that the application has a section for you to list your membership in campus groups, honorary societies, your community service, offices held, and honors received.

The job market is tough, so you need every edge that you can get on the competition. The market is more competitive in some areas than in others, so be sure to begin research on your career plans early in your matriculation. Don't wait until your senior year!

Employers, as well as individuals serving on graduate and professional schools' selection committees, peruse applications to determine what makes candidates unique when compared to others. They want to see what tangible skills you have that will make you a

better employee or graduate school member. They are looking for leadership skills, often gained through active membership in student clubs and organizations. Leadership positions and offices help teach you interpersonal skills that can't be taught or learned in the classroom.

Can you communicate verbally and in writing? Can you work effectively with subordinates as well as superiors? In every profession imaginable, you will work with people. The better your skills, the better your chances at success in the workforce; and thus, professional promotion and advancement.

The old cliché, "What goes on outside the classroom is as important as what goes on inside the classroom," is definitely applicable when considering whether or not to make time for co-curricular involvement.

Consider the experience of running for a Student Government position in a campus-wide election. Win or lose, the experience of competition, debating, meeting deadlines and expenses, and preparing and executing an entire campaign provide a learning opportunity that is unmatched. The same opportunity is possible merely by participating in a leadership position in one of the many clubs and organizations on campus.

Looking Ahead • • • • • • • • • • • • • • •

Although you are still a few years away from graduation, it is never too soon to become familiar with the services offered by the Career Services office. Many students indicate that they are undecided about a potential major and still don't know "what they want to be when they grow up!" Career Services can help you make this important decision.

Through the System of Interactive Guidance and Information Plus (SIGI+) test offered in some Career Services offices, you can learn where your interests lie and what careers match with these interests. Professional staff is available to advise you in making a career choice, and regular workshops are offered on all aspects of career planning, interviewing, and getting a job. Do not wait until your senior year to become familiar with the services of this office!

You may have heard of another famous cliché: "It's not what you know but who you know." This statement often proves true in the job market as well as graduate and professional school admissions committees. Jobs and positions in graduate and professional programs have become so competitive that candidates need all the extras they can accumulate to get the upper hand on the competition.

Undoubtedly a strong resume is one recommended extra, and getting to know influential people is another. Make sure that you know some of your instructors and professors personally so that you can ask them to write a reference for you. By being active in campus organizations and activities, you will meet faculty, staff, and administrators who could be used as references in the future. These are individuals that can attest to your academic success, your leadership potential, and your character and other personality traits.

It is also recommended that you meet as many potential references as possible as most applications will require letters from three to five persons who know or have known you personally. In practically all situations, you will be asked to submit the names of faculty members or administrators. Faculty and administrators normally will not write letters of recommendations for students they do not know or can't remember.

As a courtesy, as you begin to write your resume, ask those individuals you want to list as references for permission to list them. You want to use people who will give you a good recommendation. If you use someone without their permission, you are taking a chance that they will give you an unfair or poor recommendation.

Throughout your life, networking (using who you know to obtain certain things) will prove vital to you personally and professionally. Making influential friends is one important "connection" that you want to get started on as soon as possible!

Another connection you should investigate are the many workshops and seminars sponsored by various departments on campus. These programs can complement your education and provide information that you won't learn in any of your classes. Academic departments offer speakers and seminars that can give added insight to particular majors. The offices responsible for health and counseling on campus provide workshops throughout the year on various topics that help to build your mental and physical health. Watch for flyers, posters, and banners on campus or read the student newspaper for listings of the many opportunities to attend any of these valuable co-curricular programs on campus.

Enjoy College! • • • • • • • • • • • • • • • •

Most importantly, don't forget to have fun! Get the most out of your college experience. Take a karate, aerobics, golf, or other athletic class. Take a class that has nothing to do with your major. It is important to broaden your knowledge. Throughout your life, you will associate with people outside your profession, and you will appreciate the ability to be conversant about topics outside your career and personal interest.

Play an intramural sport. Attend varsity athletic events at the university. Audition for a role in a play. Performing in front of an audience develops self-confidence and assists you in developing skills that can be useful for interviewing as well as making presentations as a professional. Every career involves people interaction, and the more skills you have in working well with others, the more successful you can become as a professional.

Go to a dance on campus next semester. It's a great way to meet new people. Attend a theatrical or musical production. Again, it's a way to broaden your education and enjoy campus life. Participate in Homecoming or some other major campus event. Take a non-credit class just for the fun of it.

Participate in a community service project such as Habitat for Humanity or volunteer at a hospital or other local agency. Giving your time to others is a learning experience you will appreciate and is another means of developing skills that help you to become a well-rounded individual.

Do something you've never done before! You'll find your college experience to be much more enjoyable and rewarding!

Exercise 10.1 Goal Setting Exercise

Setting goals is an important aspect of helping you determine what you need to do, not only for each day, but for the rest of your life. Setting goals and developing strategies to achieve the goals are a method of time management. You should set short-term goals for now and up to the next four years. Long-term goals comprise the time period following those four years. The following is an exercise to help you set short-term and long-term goals.

By the end of today, I hope to have accomplished the following:

1.

2.

3.

4.

5.

By the end of this week, I hope to have accomplished the following:

1.

2.

3.

4.

5.

By the end of this semester, I hope to have accomplished the following:

1.

2.

3.

4.

5.

By the end of this academic year, I hope to have accomplished the following:

1.

2.

3.

4.

5.

By the end of my undergraduate matriculation, I hope to have accomplished the following:

1.

2.

3.

4.

5.

Within five years after graduation from college, I hope to have accomplished the following:

1.

2.

3.

4.

5.

Within ten years of graduation from college, I hope to have accomplished the following:

1.

2.

3.

4.

5.

My lifelong goals include the following:

1.

2.

3.

4.

5.

INDEX